NEVEN MAGUIRE'S PERFECT IRISH CHRISTMAS

NEVEN MAGUIRE'S PERFECT IRISH CHRISTMAS

GILL BOOKS

Gill Books
Hume Avenue
Park West
Dublin 12
www.gillbooks.ie

Gill Books is an imprint of M.H. Gill and Co.

978 07171 7910 7

Compiled by Orla Broderick
Designed by Graham Thew
Photographed by Joanne Murphy www.joanne-murphy.com
Styled by Johan van der Merwe
Edited by Kristin Jensen
Indexed by Adam Pozner
Printed in Italy by L.E.G.O. SpA

This book is typeset in 9.5 on 13pt, Sofia Pro.

The paper used in this book comes from the wood pulp of managed forests. For every tree felled, at least one tree is planted, thereby renewing natural resources.

A CIP catalogue record for this book is available from the British Library.

5 4 3 2 1

Props

The Props Library:
www.thepropslibrary.com

Dedication

I want to dedicate this book to my Amelda, Connor, Lucia and my family. They make my Christmas magical and so special. I love you all dearly.

Santa's Christmas List

For many years I have had the idea to write a book for Christmas. It was at Christmas that I first got involved in the kitchen at home. My mum, Vera, was a fabulous cook, and we still use many of my Auntie Maureen's recipes. Santa came to me in the guise of Nicki Howard and gave me the chance to fulfil this long-held dream. This elf is very thankful.

Orla Broderick who was, once again, chief elf in getting this book over the line in time. The styling was done by Johan van der Merwe, who was in charge of party decorations, along with Graham Thew, who designed the cover, and Joanne Murphy who did the photography. Thank you also to Kristin Jensen, who edited the manuscript. The Gill Books team, especially Catherine Gough and Teresa Daly, were once again a pleasure to work with.

A very big thank you to Claire Beasley who managed and organised the food and recipe testing. I am lucky to have you as my right-hand woman in the cookery school. Thank you to Petra Klacanska, Pamela Doherty, Raimonda Slevinskiele and Peter Comiskey, who had the very onerous task of testing and eating Christmas recipes in June. Thankfully there were no complaints!

No Christmas party would be complete without Billy Keady on camera, Ray de Brún on sound, David Hare directing and RTÉ's Brian Walsh, who is always so supportive of my television programmes.

A big season's greetings to the many presenters who have been so good to me over the years: Marty Whelan, Mary Kennedy, Marian Finucane, Brendan O'Connor, Ryan Tubridy, Ray D'Arcy, Ian Dempsey, Aine Lawlor and Pat Kenny for a start. What a talented bunch of people to have had the opportunity to work with.

Thanks to Mary Tallent Phelan, Brigid O'Dea and John Masterson. The Purcell Masterson office is my Lapland all year round! Thanks also to Colm Bradley from Hype & Holler who will look after social media with a festive flourish.

Back at Santa's Grotto in Blacklion, the extended family are what makes MacNean House & Restaurant and the Neven Maguire Cookery School what I always dreamt they could be.

I hugely appreciate the daily advice of Kieran McGovern and Andrea Doherty. Thanks to Bláithin McCabe, our restaurant manager and sommelier. To Glen Wheeler and Carmel McGirr, the two rocks in my kitchen, thank you both for your friendship and loyalty.

Thanks to Bord Bia, especially Hylda Adams, for their continued support, and best of luck to Tara McCarthy – I look forward to working with you.

Thanks to *The Irish Farmers Journal* and the combined talent of Mairead Lavery, David Leydon, Joe Lenehan and Rosie McCormack. I always enjoy writing for you.

Thanks to John Rooney and Eoin O'Flynn from Flogas, and my brother Kenneth Maguire, who is doing a fabulous job running my demos. Thanks also to Austin Duignan from Donegal Rapeseed Oil.

This has been my first full year working with the wonderful Simply Better team at Dunnes Stores. Thanks to Diarmuid Murphy, Daragh Lawless and Margaret and Anne Heffernan, who could not be more supportive.

I can think of no greater pleasure than spending Christmas Day cooking for Amelda, Connor and Lucia; Amelda's parents, Brian and Eileen; my brothers and sisters, Kenneth, Sharon, Sonya, David, Naomi, Suzanne, Alan and Karlous, and all of their partners and children. I feel very lucky to have a large and close family around me at Christmas.

Christmas comes once a year, but I hope you will find recipes in here that will give you a little taste of the festive spirit throughout the year.

Happy Christmas!
Neven

Contents

Stuffings, Sides and Sauces

Traditional Christmas Desserts

PART 3: THE HOLIDAY SEASON
Breakfasts and Brunches

St Stephen's Day and Leftovers

Party Bites

Christmas Drinks

Introduction

Christmas in our house has always been a wonderful time. It evokes the happiest of memories and I always try to recreate the nostalgia by embracing the traditions that I learned as a child.

Each year my parents would be inundated with requests to open the restaurant for Christmas dinner. However, there was never any discussion needed as it was always a given that Christmas Day was a family day and the restaurant was closed for business. This is a tradition that I am glad to continue. To me, Christmas is all about sharing precious time with family, making memories and, of course, enjoying plenty of good food!

As a youngster, the Christmas season started shortly after Halloween when Mum would start baking Christmas cakes. The smells of nutmeg and cinnamon, and the 'Christmas spirit' wafting around the house, was our first indication that Christmas was just around the corner. Mum normally made 10 to 12 Christmas cakes, so she welcomed all the help she could get! This is where I learned how to knife the cake and how to decorate it. My Auntie Maureen would take charge of the plum puddings and the mincemeat for her legendary mince pies – these are the recipes I use to this day.

Mum was a very thoughtful and giving person. For her, Christmas was most definitely a time of giving – she made lots and lots of gifts for friends and neighbours. On Christmas Eve, when my brothers and I went around the village to deliver these homemade gifts, she would usually include a special batch of mince pies. The Gardaí in the local station opposite the restaurant were always remembered on Christmas Day, too: she would send over a baked Alaska. Although we were a big family, Mum would never hear of anyone spending Christmas on their own or not having a Christmas dinner, so there would always be enough food to feed an army! It is so important to think of others, particularly at Christmastime, and this is a tradition that I hold close to my heart and I love to continue.

Christmas for us nowadays, like for many others, starts with *The Late Late Toy Show*. We don our Christmas PJs and cosy up with the twins in front of a big fire with hot chocolate and mince pies. Then that's it – mad excitement all the way until the 24th!

Like Christmas Eve when we were growing up, we follow in our parents' footsteps, calling in to neighbours and bringing a nice gift. Our children come with us and, hopefully, they will continue the tradition and make as many wonderful memories of Christmas as I have. That night, we go to midnight mass and pay homage to our loved ones and endeavour to make our own magical memories for the twins.

The arrival of Santy always brings out the child in us. We were never allowed downstairs before it got bright outside, as apparently Blacklion was Santy's last stop and there was a chance that he could still be there! So we all gathered in my parents' room and Dad would lead us down. This could often take half an hour, as Dad loved to dramatise the event. When we eventually got into the living room, total mayhem would ensue. Santy was so clever to put our names on our toys, but I could never quite understand how he could navigate the world yet never manage to spell my name correctly – NevIn? There are some things you never forget! This is another tradition that I like to continue, but I always try to make sure that Santy gets the spelling right.

Did I mention that Christmas dinner is a big deal in our house? I have cooked for up to 40 people and loved every second of it. The more the merrier in my book. I have four brothers and four sisters who have all gone on to have families of their own. There are 17 nieces and nephews and we always try to get together over Christmas. It is magical and often a little crazy, so organisation is key. My advice is simple: copy what the big man does himself by making a list and checking it twice!

Know what you're doing. Be prepared. Don't get caught on the hop. Find out in advance if any of your guests are vegetarian or have any other dietary requirements, for example. Most importantly, don't be afraid to delegate. Last year, we all mucked in: my sisters did the starters, I did the main course and we shared the desserts. Growing up, my twin brother, David, would serve the dinner. He was smart – he knew that if you served, you didn't have to do the washing up! It took a while, but we eventually cottoned on to his tactics. Now we all get stuck in so that we can relax together. Don't be afraid to give out tasks and make things ahead of time. The last thing people want is a fabulous meal, but an exhausted and grumpy host.

From our family to yours, we wish you a very Merry Christmas!

Neven (with an E!)

PART 1

*

CHRISTMAS DAY SURVIVAL GUIDE

*

Christmas Lunch Menu

This is the menu I plan to serve this Christmas. If you would prefer to serve a vegetarian option as a first course, the chestnut and wild mushroom soup (page 21) is a good one to consider. To follow, we always like to have a nice selection of desserts to choose from.

However much planning you decide to do in advance, remember to keep calm and enjoy the day. It's a good idea to delegate getting the vegetables ready, sorting out drinks and setting out nibbles. Designate a kitchen assistant and use them as an extra pair of hands – a barman, turkey carver, a rubbish collector (the kids love doing this) and most importantly, a dishwasher. As long as everyone enjoys themselves you've done a good job, so don't worry too much if something doesn't turn out perfectly, and whatever you do, don't draw everyone's attention to it. And make sure that you get to sit down and relax during the course of the day – nobody likes a martyr!

Suggested Lunch Menu

Smoked salmon
and cream cheese stacks

***

Buttermilk brined roast crown
of turkey with lemon and tarragon

Ham with sticky apricot
and ginger glaze

Apricot and sage stuffing balls

Prunes and sausages
wrapped in bacon

Perfect Christmas gravy

Creamy bread sauce

Cranberry sauce

Golden crunch roast potatoes

Braised red cabbage
with pomegranate

Celeriac and sweet potato boulangère
(doubles up as a vegetarian option)

Braised peas with bacon

***

Auntie Maureen's plum pudding

MacNean frangipane mince pies
with brandy butter

Vera's sherry trifle

Christmas cake

***

Mint chocolate truffles
and coffee

Countdown to Christmas

What follows is a countdown for the Christmas lunch menu that I've suggested – it's what I plan to do at home this year.

Things that can be in the freezer
If you are super organised, it's a great feeling to have started the Christmas preparations early. The following recipes can be frozen up to three weeks in advance of Christmas Day.
- Creamy bread sauce
- Cranberry sauce
- Apricot and sage stuffing balls
- Sausages and prunes wrapped in bacon
- Braised red cabbage with pomegranate
- Christmas pudding
- MacNean frangipane mince pies
- Brandy butter

Things that can be done more than a week before
- Make the Christmas pudding and Christmas cake up to two months in advance.
- Make the mint chocolate truffles up to two weeks in advance.
- Order your turkey and ham well in advance, along with any other specialist items.
- Shop for all the store cupboard ingredients and alcohol you'll need. Remember to think about exciting non-alcoholic mocktails for kids and designated drivers. It's always worth having extra lemons and limes, rapeseed and olive oil, eggs and a few extra loaves of bread for the freezer. Supplies of extra-wide foil, kitchen roll, cling film, parchment and greaseproof paper are also essential.
- Clean out the fridge and reorganise it so that you'll have plenty of room. Consider keeping vegetables and other unopened items in a cupboard or in the garage if it's nice and cool.
- Go through the crockery, cutlery, glasses and table decorations you want to use.
- Make extra ice or buy it in a bag.
- Make a food shopping list of everything you think you'll need and keep it handy so that you can add to it as you think of things.
- Make a list of things to do that is well spaced out.
- Sharpen your knives.

On 23 December
- Do your final shop and pick up the turkey and ham.
- Make turkey stock, cool and strain.
- Put the turkey into the buttermilk brine and calculate the cooking time.
- Soak the gammon in water for at least 8 hours or overnight and calculate the cooking time. This can be cooked overnight with great success or have it ready to be done first thing on the 24th.
- Make the celeriac and sweet potato boulangère.
- Ice the Christmas cake and store as instructed.

On 24 December
- If the ham has not been cooked overnight, then put it on early in the morning, roughly 14 hours before you intend to eat it. So if you're planning on an 8pm dinner, the ham needs to be switched on at 6am.

- Make the smoked salmon and cream cheese stacks.
- Make the sherry trifle.
- Cook the ham with sticky apricot and ginger glaze and eat some of it for dinner with braised red cabbage with pomegranate and jacket potatoes topped with sour cream and chives.
- Peel the potatoes and keep them covered in water.
- Take the butter out of the fridge to soften for the turkey.
- Leave all frozen items out in a cool place overnight to defrost.
- Chill down all the drinks you might need for the day.
- Set the table and do any last-minute tidying up.

Christmas Day (served at 3pm)
The timings I have given for Christmas lunch are based on a 1.8kg (4lb) turkey crown.

11.30am Take the turkey out of the brine and bring back to room temperature before cooking. Arrange the oven shelves so that everything you need to cook will fit.

12.30pm Preheat the oven to 190°C (375°F/ gas mark 5) and finish preparing the turkey for the oven. Unless you have a second oven to cook the celeriac and sweet potato boulangère in, bake it in advance, then leave at room temperature covered with foil.

12.50pm Put the turkey in the oven for 1 hour 40 minutes. Carve as much of the ham as you think you are going to need and put it in a shallow ovenproof dish. Cover with foil and leave to come back to room temperature.

1.45pm Prepare the roast potatoes so they are ready to go into the oven at 2pm.

2.20pm Arrange the smoked salmon and cream cheese stacks on plates for the first course and put on the table. Cover the plates with cling film if you think the room is very warm.

2.30pm Take the turkey out of the oven and put in a warm place to rest, loosely covered with foil and a clean tea towel. Put the prunes and sausages wrapped in bacon in the oven. Finish making the gravy. Reheat the red cabbage in a second oven at 180°C (350°F/gas mark 4) or reheat gently on the hob in a covered pan or in the microwave.

2.40pm Put the apricot and sage stuffing balls in the oven along with the carved ham and the celeriac and sweet potato boulangère to warm through. Put plates and any serving dishes in the oven to warm.

2.45pm Make the braised peas with bacon and heat the bread sauce and gravy on the hob or in the microwave.

2.50pm Carve the turkey and remove everything from the ovens so that you can serve up on the warmed plates and serving dishes.

Later Reheat mince pies and the Christmas pudding. Finish the trifle for serving and don't forget the mint chocolate truffles tucked away in the fridge!

How to Cook for a Large Group

I love giving parties at Christmastime and often find myself cooking for large crowds at home, which can require a good deal of planning, early shopping and cooking in advance. This is all vital if you want to have time to chat and have a drink with the people you have invited. Most of the recipes in this book are for six to eight people, but they can be easily doubled (or trebled) to serve more if you are organising a really big get-together. Remember, though, that if you have more guests than you have chairs, you will have to serve foods capable of being eaten with a fork, such as the salmon coulibiac (page 147), barley risotto (page 158) or one-pot harissa turkey and butternut squash curry (page 124).

To save you time and last-minute work, most of the recipes here can be prepared or cooked some time in advance. Make sure to cool bulk-cooked food quickly before putting it in the fridge. The best thing to do is to sit down one evening when you've time to relax and work out the menu. Consider serving most dishes cold as part of a buffet, but it's sensible to keep your choices restricted. It's better to have a lot of a few things than a little of too many. It's also worth bearing in mind that the more people there are, the less food they eat per head. If you don't fancy cooking at all, I find that attractively laid out antipasti platters with spiced nuts and marinated olives (page 192) always go down well. Consider putting breadsticks in jars and regular French baguettes in vases for dramatic effect.

A paella (page 152) can look spectacular if you've got a large enough pan to do it in. I also find that porchetta with sautéed potatoes always goes a long way and all ovens will take double the size of the recipe on page 144, which would feed up to 24 people for a sit-down lunch. For dessert I have a wonderful selection of cakes and other desserts that could all be successfully made the day before you need them.

Above all, remember that a Christmas party is the best sort to give. For one thing, everyone is already in the festive spirit and is out to enjoy themselves. I find the less stressed you are, the better the party will be, so make sure all the drinks you need are going to be chilled on time and give yourself enough time to get ready, then take a deep breath and open the door with your best smile.

Top Tips for a Stress-free Christmas

Shop ahead

If you are wondering how early you can pick up the turkey, they should be bought on or after 22 December. Ideally you should order your turkey well in advance, then the right size will be waiting for you at the supermarket or butcher until you need to collect it.

What type of turkey to buy

I prefer to use a free-range or organic bird for this special occasion. Work out the size you need or ask your butcher for advice on this. Make sure they weigh it for you so that you can easily work out how long to cook it for (see the timings on page 14). When you get home, remove the turkey from the packaging and remove the giblets – it's best to make the stock the day you pick it up. Put the turkey on a tray and cover with greaseproof paper. Store in the bottom of the fridge.

Cooking for one: Turkey breast

If you are only cooking for yourself and would like some leftovers or for just two people, a single turkey breast is a good option. If you have the time and inclination it would benefit from soaking in a buttermilk brine (see page 37) for a more tender and moist texture, but it's not essential. Ask your butcher for a 350g (12oz) turkey breast and heat a sauté pan over a low heat. Add 25g (1oz) of butter, and when it's foaming, add the turkey breast, turning it in the butter, but don't

allow it to colour. Cover with a round of parchment paper and the lid. Cook for 5–7 minutes on each side, until just cooked through and tender. Carve into thin slices and arrange slightly overlapping on a plate to serve.

Is the turkey cooked?

Ovens can vary, especially when you are cooking other things at the same time and opening the door regularly. Work out the approximate time to cook your turkey (see page 14), but it's essential to test that it's done, ideally with a meat thermometer or skewer. Insert the dial/spike type of thermometer into the thickest part of the thigh at the beginning of cooking or use a digital meat thermometer or a skewer to check the temperature at the end of cooking. I always cook mine to 75–80°C (167–176°F) rather than the 90°C (194°F) often suggested on some thermometer gauges. To test whether the turkey is cooked with a skewer, insert it into the thickest part of the thigh and check the juices – they should run clear. If the juices are still pink, then the turkey is not yet cooked. Put it back in the oven, checking it every 10 minutes, and cover your vegetable sides with foil. When the turkey is ready to carve, simply reheat the veg – microwave any that are steamed or boiled and pop the roasted vegetables in a high oven for 5 minutes.

Resting the turkey

You should leave a turkey to rest for about 30 minutes, although a whole turkey will sit for up to 2 hours if you get terribly behind or someone is delayed. Lift it out of the roasting tin with the help of the foil and put on a platter. Cover loosely with foil and a clean tea towel. This allows the juices to settle back into the meat, leaving it deliciously moist and easier to carve.

Carving made easy

For neat slices, make sure your carving knife is sharp. No carving knife? Use a long, thin-bladed knife or electric carving knife instead. Don't use a serrated knife, as this will rip the meat.

Once the turkey has rested, transfer it to a large board. Hold one of the legs by the knuckle between the leg and body (the hip joint), pulling the leg away from the body as you go. The leg should come away quite easily. Repeat with the other leg and then either carve each leg between the thigh and the drumstick to create two pieces or slice the meat straight off the legs. Discard the bones or freeze for later to use in stock.

To carve the breast meat, the traditional method is to hold your knife flat against the breast, securing the bird with a carving fork, and cut the meat along the length of the breast. The other option is to cut the entire breast off the carcass by slicing down one side of the entire backbone, then cutting under the breast, following the line of the ribcage. Then just slice the breast on the board and repeat with the other side.

Hot Christmas dinner

Warm the plates in a low oven (the microwave or even the dishwasher works too) and put the turkey and ham on the plates first, followed by stuffing and any garnishes. Finish with the vegetables and roast potatoes. Alternatively, create a buffet area and allow everyone to help themselves, perhaps getting parents to help any children with their selections first. Have cutlery to hand, wrapped in napkins.

Turkey cooking chart

Note that the cooking times for the salt-rubbed turkey with sage and orange on page 40 is a slightly different technique, as the legs and wings are confited and the crown is cooked on the bone separately. I always preheat the oven to 190°C (375°F/gas mark 5). Make sure your turkey has been allowed to come back to room temperature. If you have stuffed it you will need to weigh the stuffing and add that amount to your turkey weight. Allow 20 minutes per 450g (1lb) plus 20 minutes extra.

- **1.8kg (4lb) turkey crown (off the bone) will take 1 hour 40 minutes**

- **2kg (4½lb) turkey crown (off the bone) will take 1 hour 50 minutes**

- **4.5kg (10lb) oven-ready turkey will take 3 hours 40 minutes**

- **5.4kg (12lb) oven-ready turkey will take 4 hours 20 minutes**

Christmas Drinks Recommended by Blaithín McCabe, Sommelier at MacNean House & Restaurant

Christmas season is party time, and what better way to enjoy company than with the right tipple? I always get asked what wine and drinks are recommended for the festivities, so I would like to share some of my suggestions with you.

On the first day of Christmas my sommelier said to me …
On a frosty night, spiced cider is a great alternative to mulled wine. The smell of cinnamon and nutmeg is such a comfort. For a non-alcoholic version, use spiced apple juice.

Try infusing a little lemongrass, root ginger and honey in your favourite hot toddy or try my Irish whiskey punch on page 222. Remember: don't use Dad's rare whiskey – save that for drinking neat! A basic whiskey or port will suffice for hot drinks.

Choosing wine for a range of palates can be tricky. Choose grape varietal blends that are not too one dimensional, unless you know your guests very well. Usually the first grape listed on the bottle is the dominant variety. In Ireland we are blessed with a range of well-priced wines, which are available in the off trade.

Keep pre-dinner/lunch drinks crisp and fresh to tantalise the taste buds. Try drier styles of white wines, such as unoaked Chardonnays, or gins with more citrus botanicals. A chilled fino sherry is great with nuts and nibbles.

At least once a year spoil yourself with Champagne, the ultimate celebration drink. Choose a Blanc de Blanc for great freshness or one with more Pinot Noir and yeasty complexity to complement food.

Chablis, Sancerre and Pinot Blanc work well with lighter seafood dishes. Foie gras and game starters are best served with Gewürztraminer or aromatic white grape varieties.

The classic match for turkey and ham is Pinot Noir. Pinot Noirs from the Southern Hemisphere are more fruit driven; Burgundian styles are more delicate and have a more savoury, earthy flavour. Beaujolais reds such as Moulin-à-Vent and Côtes de Brouilly have more summer fruit flavours and complement lighter meat dishes. Duck and goose are richer, so Crianzas and Ripassas have more ripe dark fruits and a touch more spice.

For those avoiding red wine, heavier oaked whites from Burgundy and California or barrel-fermented whites from Bordeaux are a real treat. These wines are much more complex for roasted poultry recipes. Puligny Montrachet is one of Neven's favourite white wines at Christmas.

Cheese, please, but where's my port? LBV ports are richer in dark fruit flavours. If you prefer a nuttier style, tawny ports have had some oxidation, which contributes to a distinctive flavour. Try one slightly chilled. Blue cheeses require sweetness, so they are a particularly good match with port.

Banyuls from Provence is another fortified wine that is great with Christmas pudding and chocolate- or coffee-based desserts. Drizzle some PX sherry over some ice cream – dessert in seconds! Late harvest Riesling/Pinot Gris are lighter in style than traditional dessert wines and complement fruit-based desserts. Choose Sauternes for crumbles and richer desserts.

A log fire is so inviting for a rich red wine, but choose wisely. Consider if the wine is to be served with or without food. Heavier Shirazs and reds high in tannins are best with food. They usually require some decanting and time to breathe. Fruitier reds will be softer on the palate. Indulge in hot chocolate made with Cointreau or crème de menthe, and don't forget the marshmallows!

Most importantly, enjoy the craic, remember to keep hydrated and experiment with different styles of drinks and wine. Sláinte!

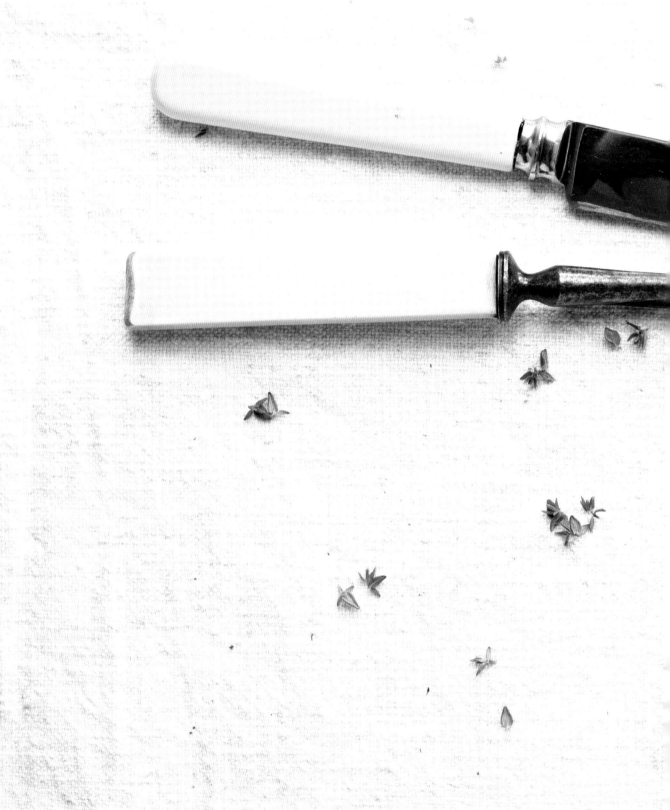

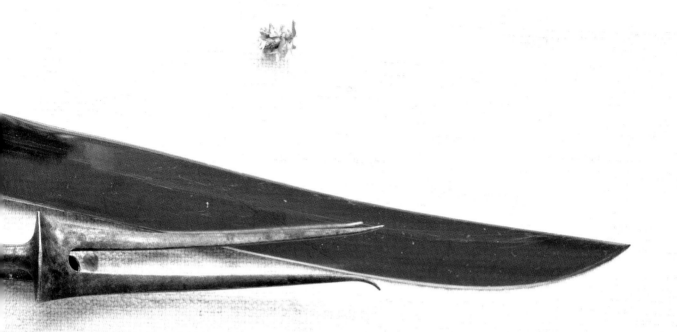

PART 2

**

THE PERFECT CHRISTMAS DINNER

**

**

SOUPS & STARTERS

**

Chestnut & Wild Mushroom Soup

This is one of my all-time favourite soups, particularly at Christmas, when vac-packed chestnuts are readily available. If you want to keep the soup vegetarian, leave out the smoked duck and garnish with some sautéed mushrooms instead. It can be made up to three days in advance and kept covered in the fridge. It can also be frozen for up to one month but may need to be blitzed with a hand-held blender when reheating, as it may split.

SERVES 4–8

50g (2oz) dried mixed wild mushrooms

1 tbsp rapeseed oil

450g (1lb) peeled chestnuts (canned or vacuum-packed), chopped

100g (4oz) smoked duck, thinly sliced

1 large onion, finely chopped

1 tsp chopped fresh thyme

1.2 litres (2 pints) chicken or vegetable stock

200ml (7fl oz) cream

sea salt and freshly ground black pepper

snipped fresh chives, to garnish

fresh micro herbs, to garnish

1 Put the dried wild mushrooms in a heatproof bowl and pour 400ml (14fl oz) of boiling water over to cover. Set aside for 20 minutes, until they have plumped up. Drain the mushrooms and gently squeeze dry, reserving the soaking liquid.

2 Heat a large pan and add the oil. Add the chestnuts, half of the smoked duck, the onion and drained wild mushrooms and sweat gently for 10 minutes, until golden brown, stirring occasionally. Season to taste.

3 Add the thyme to the pan with the reserved soaking liquid and the stock, stirring to combine. Bring to the boil, then reduce the heat and simmer for another 20 minutes. Stir in the cream and allow to heat through for 1 minute, then whizz with a hand-held blender until as smooth as possible. Season to taste, then blend again until light and foamy, tilting the pan to get the maximum effect.

4 To serve, ladle the soup into warmed bowls. Garnish each one with the rest of the smoked duck, the chives and micro herbs.

Lobster Bisque

This is an extremely rich soup, so only serve it in small amounts if you want your guests to have any room left for other courses! You can substitute the lobster for crab for a less intense flavour.

SERVES 4–6

350g (12oz) frozen cooked lobster, thawed

1 tbsp rapeseed oil

50g (2oz) butter

1 small onion, diced

1 carrot, diced

1 celery stick, diced

½ small fennel bulb, diced

1 fresh bouquet garni

4 ripe tomatoes, quartered

4 tbsp brandy (Cognac if possible)

2 tsp tomato purée

900ml (1½ pints) fish stock

150ml (¼ pint) dry white wine

sea salt and freshly ground black pepper

lightly whipped cream, to garnish

fresh micro herbs, to garnish

1 Cut the lobster in half lengthways, then open it up and remove the tail meat, removing and discarding the intestinal tract and stomach. Twist and remove the claws, then using the back of a knife, crack the claws and remove the meat. Chop the tail and claw meat and reserve. Put the shell in a polythene bag and smash into small pieces.

2 Heat the oil and half of the butter in a large pan and stir in the onion, carrot, celery and fennel. Add the lobster shell and bouquet garni, then cover and cook for 10–15 minutes, until the vegetables are softened.

3 Add the tomatoes and cook for 5 minutes, then increase the heat and pour in the brandy – it should reduce immediately. Add the tomato purée, stock and wine and bring to a simmer, then cook gently for 30 minutes, until slightly reduced. Season to taste.

4 Pass the soup through a fine sieve into a bowl, then ladle into a food processor. Add the remaining butter and the reserved lobster meat, reserving some to garnish. Whizz until blended, then return to a clean pan. Reheat gently, then ladle into bowls and add a quenelle of the whipped cream to each one. Finish with a small mound of the reserved lobster meat and a sprinkling of the micro herbs to serve.

Leek & Potato Soup with Smoked Trout

This soup can be served hot or chilled, depending on what suits. However, it's worth remembering that cold food needs to be highly seasoned to bring out the best flavours.

SERVES 4–6

1 tbsp rapeseed oil

2 potatoes, peeled and cut into cubes

1 onion, finely chopped

3 small leeks, finely chopped

1 tbsp chopped fresh thyme

900ml (1½ pints) chicken or vegetable stock

150ml (¼ pint) cream

pinch of freshly grated nutmeg

sea salt and freshly ground black pepper

crème fraîche, to garnish

thin strips of smoked trout, to garnish

snipped fresh chives, to garnish

1. Heat the oil in a large pan set over a medium heat, then tip in the potatoes and onion. Cook for 5 minutes, stirring constantly. Add the leeks and thyme and cook for another 5 minutes, stirring occasionally, until all the vegetables have softened but not coloured.

2. Pour the stock into the pan and bring to the boil. Reduce the heat, then cover the pan and simmer for 20 minutes, until slightly reduced and all the vegetables are completely tender.

3. Blitz the soup with a hand-held blender, then pour in the cream. Season to taste and add the nutmeg, then reheat gently.

4. Ladle the soup into warmed bowls and garnish with dollops of crème fraîche, a few strips of smoked trout and a sprinkling of snipped fresh chives or serve chilled (see the introduction above).

Roasted Cauliflower Soup with Seared Scallops

This soup tastes so creamy and decadent that everyone is bound to love it. Roasting the cauliflower brings out the nuttiness and enhances and intensifies the flavour. It can be made up to three days in advance and kept covered in the fridge. The sweet scallops are a perfect partner and will have all your guests begging for the recipe!

SERVES 4–6

1 medium cauliflower (about 900g (2lb))

2 shallots, cut into quarters

3 tbsp rapeseed oil, plus a little extra

4 garlic cloves, unpeeled

900ml (1½ pints) vegetable stock

300ml (½ pint) milk

4–6 scallops, well dried on kitchen paper

sea salt and freshly ground black pepper

fresh pea shoots, to garnish (optional)

1 Preheat the oven to 200°C (400°F/gas mark 6). Line a large baking sheet with non-stick baking paper.

2 Trim the cauliflower into florets, discarding the leaves and tough stalk. Spread the florets on the baking sheet with the shallots and toss with 2 tablespoons of the oil. Season to taste.

3 Wrap the garlic cloves, along with a drizzle of oil and pinch of salt, in a piece of tin foil and put on the baking sheet with the vegetables. The garlic will roast perfectly this way, making it nice and soft, which is exactly what you want.

4 Roast in the oven for 30–35 minutes, until the cauliflower has started to brown around the edges, stirring once halfway through. Remove from the oven and leave to cool a little, then transfer to a food processor with the peeled garlic cloves, stock and milk and blend until smooth.

5 When ready to serve, reheat the cauliflower soup in a pan set over a medium heat.

6 To cook the scallops, heat the remaining tablespoon of oil in a non-stick frying pan set over a high heat. Season the scallops with some salt, then sear for about 20 seconds on each side, until golden brown and nicely caramelised. Ideally they should be slightly undercooked in the middle. You may need to do this in batches depending on the size of your pan.

7 To serve, ladle the roasted cauliflower soup into bowls and garnish with the scallops and pea shoots (if using).

Sizzling Dublin Bay Prawns with Chorizo & Garlic

Dublin Bay prawns actually look a lot like small slender lobsters, with rather more delicate colouring and lighter claws in relation to the body. They may seem like an expensive luxury but are well worth every cent, especially for a special occasion like Christmas.

SERVES 4

20 large Dublin Bay prawns

4 tbsp rapeseed oil

knob of butter

50g (2oz) cooking chorizo, peeled and finely diced

1 mild fresh red chilli, halved, deseeded and cut into rings

1 garlic clove, thinly sliced

½ lemon, pips removed

1 tbsp chopped fresh flat-leaf parsley

sea salt and freshly ground black pepper

crusty bread, to serve

1 To prepare the prawns, firmly twist the head away from the body and discard or use for stock. Turn each prawn over and crack open the hard shell along the belly, then carefully peel it away from the flesh, twisting off the tail. To remove the intestinal tract, which looks like a thin black vein running down the back of the prawn flesh, run the tip of a small knife down the back of each prawn, then lift up and pull out the vein. If you are lucky sometimes the vein comes away with the prawn tail or it can be easily pulled out without having to cut the prawn at all.

2 Heat the oil in a large frying pan set over a high heat with the knob of butter. Once the butter has stopped foaming, add the chorizo and sauté for a few minutes, until sizzling. Add the chilli and garlic and sauté for another 30 seconds, until the garlic is lightly golden.

3 Tip the prepared prawns into the pan and sauté for another few minutes, until tender. The prawns will change colour and begin to curl up. Be careful not to overcook. Add a good squeeze of lemon juice and sprinkle over the parsley, tossing to coat. Season to taste.

4 Divide among warmed dishes with all their delicious juices. Serve at once with plenty of crusty bread.

Smoked Salmon & Cream Cheese Stacks

This is a great starter to have on Christmas Day as it can be made well in advance and will sit happily in the fridge for up to 8 hours. Everyone loves the combination of smoked salmon and brown bread, and this is something just a wee bit different.

SERVES 4–6

1 x 200g (7oz) tub of cream cheese

2 tbsp finely diced cucumber (peeled and seeded)

1 tbsp finely diced radish

1 tbsp snipped fresh chives

2 tsp horseradish sauce

1 tsp prepared English mustard

12–18 slices of brown soda bread (each about 3–5mm (⅛–¼in) thick)

1 x 200g (7oz) packet of smoked salmon slices

sea salt and freshly ground white pepper

lightly dressed mixed salad leaves, to garnish

For the pickled red onion:

4 tbsp rice wine vinegar

2 tbsp caster sugar

1 red onion, cut into fine wedges

1 Put the cream cheese in a bowl and mix in the cucumber, radish, chives, horseradish sauce and mustard. Season to taste.

2 Stamp or cut out rounds from the soda bread that are each about 6cm (2¼in) in diameter – you'll need three for each stack. Repeat with the smoked salmon.

3 To make the pickled red onion, put the vinegar in a bowl and stir in the sugar to dissolve. Add the onion wedges and toss to coat. Cover with cling film and set aside for at least 10 minutes, or up to 8 hours is fine.

4 To serve, place a round of soda bread on each plate. Top each one with 1 tablespoon of the cream cheese mixture, followed by a round of smoked salmon. Repeat until you have three layers in each stack. Add a spoonful of the pickled red onion and garnish with the salad to serve.

Chicken Liver Parfait

The parfait can be made four days in advance and kept in the fridge.
I love it with the grape chutney on page 181 and I like to serve it with
toasted brioche and a salad.

SERVES 8

400g (14oz) fresh chicken livers, well trimmed

300ml (½ pint) milk

100g (4oz) unsalted butter, softened

3 shallots, finely chopped

1 garlic clove, crushed

1 tsp chopped fresh thyme

1 tbsp ruby red port

5 eggs

1 tbsp cream

sea salt and freshly ground black pepper

grape chutney (page 181), to serve

1 Soak the chicken livers in the milk overnight. The next day, drain and dry with kitchen paper. Blend in a food processor for 2–3 minutes, until very smooth.

2 Preheat the oven to 180°C (350°F/gas mark 4).

3 Melt a knob of the butter in a sauté pan set over a low heat and sweat the shallots, garlic and thyme for 4–5 minutes to soften but not colour. Add the port and cook for 1 minute. Remove from the heat to cool a little, then add to the chicken liver purée with the eggs, cream, the rest of the butter and plenty of seasoning. Blend again for 30 seconds.

4 Pass through a fine sieve into a jug, then pour into 8 x 120ml (4fl oz) Kilner jars. Cover each one with tin foil and place in a bain-marie (a roasting tin half-filled with boiling water) and cook in the oven 20 minutes, until they still have a slight wobble in the centre. Remove from the bain-marie and take off the foil, then leave to cool. Seal and chill until needed.

5 Arrange the Kilner jars on plates with the grape chutney to serve.

Crispy Goats' Cheese with Roasted Beetroot, Cranberries, Watercress & Caramelised Walnuts

This is a great vegetarian starter. It's worth seeking out a good-quality Irish goats' cheese such as Corleggy or Ryefield.

SERVES 4

50g (2oz) fresh white breadcrumbs

2 tbsp finely chopped fresh flat-leaf parsley

2 tsp toasted pine nuts, finely chopped

2 tsp sesame seeds

2 eggs

50g (2oz) plain flour

4 x 4cm (1½in) thick slices of goats' cheese (from a log with a 7.5cm (3in) diameter)

groundnut oil, for deep-frying

100g (4oz) fresh watercress

50g (2oz) dried cranberries

juice of ½ lemon

For the roasted beetroot:

675g (1½lb) small beetroot, scrubbed and tops trimmed (each about 75g (3oz))

2 sprigs of fresh thyme

4 tbsp balsamic vinegar

2 tbsp rapeseed oil, plus extra for the dressing

For the caramelised walnuts:

2 tbsp butter

100g (4oz) walnut halves

2 tbsp maple syrup

sea salt and freshly ground black pepper

1 Put the breadcrumbs in a shallow dish and mix with the parsley, nuts, sesame seeds and seasoning. Beat the eggs in a separate dish and season lightly. Put the flour on a plate and season. Lightly coat the goats' cheese in the seasoned flour, then dip into the beaten egg, shaking off any excess. Finally, coat in the breadcrumb mixture. Chill on a tray lined with parchment paper for at least 30 minutes (or overnight is fine) to firm up.

2 To roast the beetroot, preheat the oven to 220°C (425°F/gas mark 7). Put the beetroot in a roasting tin with the thyme and drizzle over the balsamic vinegar and oil. Season, then cover with tin foil and roast in the oven for 1 hour, until the beets can be pierced easily with a knife. Leave to cool, then cut into quarters and toss back into the cooking juices.

3 To caramelise the walnuts, melt the butter in a frying pan set over a medium–high heat. Add the walnuts and toss to coat, then drizzle over the maple syrup and stir for a minute or two, until caramelised. Spread on a piece of parchment paper to cool.

4 Reduce the oven temperature to 180°C (350°F/gas mark 4). Heat the groundnut oil in a deep-sided pan or deep-fat fryer to 180°C (350°F) and cook the coated goats' cheese for 3 minutes, until crisp and golden brown. Drain well, then put on a baking sheet lined with non-stick baking paper and bake in the oven for another 3–4 minutes to completely heat through.

5 Meanwhile, arrange the watercress on plates with the cranberries and lightly dress with rapeseed oil and some lemon juice. Scatter the roasted beetroot on top with the caramelised walnuts and finish each one with a piece of crispy goats' cheese.

THE MAIN EVENT

Buttermilk Brined Roast Crown of Turkey with Lemon and Tarragon

A great alternative to roasting a large bird, the crown is the turkey breasts and wing joints with the legs removed. From feedback this is the most popular recipe I've ever done, as the buttermilk brine ensures that the flesh stays wonderfully succulent.

SERVES 6–8

1 x 1.8–2kg (4–4½lb) turkey crown, off the bone

75g (3oz) butter, softened

1 garlic clove, crushed

finely grated rind of 1 lemon

1 tbsp chopped fresh flat-leaf parsley

2 tsp chopped fresh tarragon

4 rindless smoked bacon rashers

For the buttermilk brine:

2 litres (3½ pints) buttermilk

2 lemons, thinly sliced

1 garlic bulb, separated into cloves and sliced

15g (½oz) fresh tarragon sprigs, roughly bruised

3 tbsp sea salt or kosher salt

2 tsp freshly ground black pepper

1 Mix together all the ingredients for the buttermilk brine in a turkey bag, then add the turkey crown. Tie up the bag securely and put in the salad drawer at the bottom of the fridge – up to two days is best, but brine for at least 24 hours.

2 Preheat the oven to 190°C (375°F/gas mark 5).

3 Cream the butter until soft, then beat in the garlic, lemon rind and herbs. Remove the crown from the brine and drain off any excess liquid, then pat the skin dry with kitchen paper. Gently loosen the neck flap away from the breast and pack the flavoured butter right under the skin (this is best done using gloves on your hands). Rub the butter into the flesh, then re-cover with the skin and secure with a small skewer or sew with fine twine. Cover the top of the turkey crown with the rashers.

4 Put the prepared turkey crown in the oven and calculate your cooking time: 20 minutes per 450g (1lb) plus 20 minutes. This will cook much quicker than a whole turkey, so make sure to baste it often. You can cover it with foil if it's browning too quickly. When cooked, cover with foil to rest and keep warm. Drain away the cooking juices to make the gravy (see page 76).

5 To serve, carve the turkey crown into slices and arrange on warmed plates with a selection of your favourite accompaniments.

Roast Turkey with Streaky Bacon

This is the easiest way to roast a turkey, and fortunately, for many people it's also the best. Forget about having the time to brine it or trying to turn it over while it cooks – this method is absolutely foolproof.

SERVES 10–12

1 x 4.5–5.4kg (10–12lb) oven-ready turkey (preferably free-range), at room temperature

1 quantity stuffing (pages 66, 69, 70 or 74) (optional)

100g (4oz) butter, softened

15–18 rindless streaky bacon rashers

sea salt and freshly ground black pepper

small bunch of fresh herbs (to include parsley, sage and bay leaves), to garnish

1 Preheat the oven to 190°C (375°F/gas mark 5).

2 Turn the turkey breast side up and pack the neck cavity loosely with stuffing (if using), then tie the top of the drumsticks together with string. Smear with most of the butter and season generously, then place the bacon over the breasts to cover them completely. Weigh the turkey to calculate the required cooking time, allowing 20 minutes per 450g (1lb) plus 20 minutes extra.

3 Lay a large sheet of foil lengthways over a large roasting tin, leaving enough at each end to wrap over the turkey, then lightly butter the foil. Repeat with another sheet of foil, but this time laying it across the tin. Place the stuffed turkey in the centre of the foil, breast side up, then wrap loosely to enclose but still allowing air to circulate around the turkey.

4 Put in the oven and cook according to your calculated cooking time, carefully unwrapping and basting the turkey every 40 minutes. For the final hour, fold back and remove the foil, keeping the ends of the drumsticks still covered in foil to prevent them from burning. Baste well and return to the oven. The turkey should be a rich, dark brown colour. To make sure it's cooked, insert a fine skewer into the thickest part of the thigh – the juices should run clear, but if they are still pink, return the turkey to the oven and check again every 15 minutes, until you are happy that the turkey is cooked right through. Remove from the oven and transfer to a serving platter. Cover with foil and leave to rest in a warm place for 10 minutes (up to 30 minutes is fine).

5 To serve, garnish the turkey with the bunch of herbs in the neck cavity and bring to the table. Carve into slices and arrange on warmed plates with all the trimmings.

Salt-rubbed Turkey with Sage & Orange

This is quite a 'cheffy' recipe that takes a little more effort, but it keeps the breast of the bird really juicy while the leg meat literally falls off the bone. Ask your butcher to do all the work for you and make sure he chops the neck and backbone into pieces for gravy. But if it all sounds like too much work, just use this method with the crown.

SERVES 8–10

150g (5oz) Maldon sea salt or kosher salt

8 fresh sage leaves, chopped

2 tbsp light brown sugar

1 tbsp black peppercorns

finely grated rind of 4 oranges

1 x 5kg (11lb) turkey, legs and thighs removed and wings cut from the breast

500g (18oz) duck or goose fat

1 large onion, cut into thick slices

good handful of fresh mixed herbs, such as sage, rosemary and thyme

50g (2oz) butter, softened

1 Make the salt rub up to four days in advance. Grind the salt, sage, sugar and peppercorns in a pestle and mortar (or use the end of a rolling pin in a bowl), then stir in the orange rind. Put one-third of the salt rub into a large resealable bag and the remainder into another bag, then chill until needed. Put the legs and wings into the bag with the third of the salt rub and massage it into the skin, then leave in the fridge for 24 hours or at least overnight.

2 When you're ready to cook, preheat the oven to 120°C (250°F/gas mark ½).

3 Rinse off the salt rub and pat the legs and wings dry with kitchen paper. Put the duck or goose fat in a roasting tin large enough to just fit everything comfortably and melt in the oven for 5 minutes, then add the turkey pieces, ensuring they are submerged. Cook for 4 hours, until completely tender. Leave to cool, then cover and chill for up to three days.

4 The day before you want to eat, put the turkey crown into the other bag with the rest of the salt rub and massage it into the skin and flesh. Chill overnight.

5 One hour before you want to cook it, remove the turkey crown and rinse, then pat dry with kitchen paper. Take the legs and wings out of the fridge so that they will come easily out of the fat, then transfer to a roasting tin. You can strain out the fat to use for your roast potatoes (see page 52) if liked.

6 Preheat the oven to 190°C (375°F/gas mark 5) and line a separate roasting tin with foil.

7 Set a wire rack on top of the foil-lined roasting tin and scatter over the onion and herbs. Sit the crown on top and rub all over with the butter. Roast in the oven, uncovered, for 40 minutes, then cover with foil and cook for 30 minutes.

Remove the foil and cook for 15 minutes, until cooked through and tender. Transfer to a platter and cover with foil, then rest in a warm place for 30 minutes.

8   Meanwhile, reheat the turkey legs and wings in the oven for 30 minutes, until heated through and the skin has become nice and crispy. Add to the platter with the crown and carve into slices. Arrange on warmed plates with all the trimmings.

Prunes & Sausages
Wrapped in Bacon, p.65

Salt-rubbed Turkey with Sage & Orange, p.40

Roast Turkey with Streaky Bacon, p.38

Ham with Sticky Apricot & Ginger Glaze

This ham is a firm favourite in our house over the festive season, whether served hot or cold. It can be cooked and left in the fridge for up to a week, making it extremely handy.

SERVES 10–12

5.25kg (11½lb) leg of gammon, on the bone

4 celery sticks, roughly chopped

2 onions, sliced

5cm (2in) piece of fresh ginger, sliced

1 small bunch of fresh thyme

1 tbsp black peppercorns

4 whole cloves

2 star anise

1.5 litres (2½ pints) dry cider

1 tsp ground ginger

For the glaze:

175g (6oz) good-quality apricot jam or conserve

100g (4oz) light brown sugar

juice of 1 lemon

4 star anise

4 pieces of preserved stem ginger, cut into small matchstick-sized strips

1 Soak the gammon in cold water for at least 6 hours (or overnight is best), then drain.

2 Preheat the oven to 120°C (250°F/gas mark ½). Use a large deep roasting tin with a rack that's big enough to hold the ham. Put the celery, onions, fresh ginger, thyme, peppercorns, cloves and star anise in the tin and pour over the cider, then put the rack on top. Sit the ham on the rack and cover with a large tent of foil, sealing it well. Put on the hob over a high heat and bring to the boil. Simmer for 15 minutes, then transfer to the oven. Cook for 12 hours or overnight – you can now leave it for one or two days before finishing the recipe. Alternatively, leave to rest and cool down for at least 30 minutes.

3 Raise the oven temperature to 180°C (350°F/gas mark 4).

4 Now make the glaze. Put the apricot jam or conserve in a small pan with the brown sugar, lemon juice and star anise. Heat gently until the sugar has dissolved, then add the stem ginger and simmer for 3–4 minutes, until reduced to a thick glaze, stirring to ensure it doesn't catch at the bottom.

5 Carefully peel away the skin on the ham, leaving the layer of white fat intact. Using a sharp knife, score the fat diagonally into a diamond pattern, being careful not to cut into the meat. Put into a clean roasting tin and rub with the ground ginger, then brush the glaze on top. Roast in the oven for about 45 minutes, until golden and sticky. Transfer to a platter and leave to rest for 15–20 minutes. Carve slices from the ham and use as required, warm or cold.

Honey-glazed Ham with Cloves

This ham is cooked in the traditional manner: it's simmered in a large pan first before being finished off in the oven, which keeps the finished result really moist.

SERVES 10–12

5.25kg (11½lb) leg of gammon, on the bone and skin on

4 celery sticks, roughly chopped

2 onions, sliced

1 bunch of fresh thyme

1 tbsp black peppercorns

200ml (7fl oz) Irish whiskey

200ml (7fl oz) honey

2 tbsp redcurrant jelly

2 tbsp balsamic vinegar

1 tbsp ground allspice

2 tsp whole cloves

1 Soak the gammon in cold water for at least 6 hours (or overnight is best), then drain.

2 Weigh the gammon and calculate the cooking time, allowing 20 minutes per 450g (1lb) plus 20 minutes – this size takes about 4 hours. Put in a large pan, cover with water and bring to the boil, skimming off any scum. Add the celery, onions, thyme and peppercorns and return to the boil, then cover, reduce the heat and simmer until completely tender, occasionally skimming off any scum that rises to the top. If you aren't sure the gammon is properly cooked, check the bone end – it should come away freely from the gammon joint. Drain and leave until cool enough to handle.

3 Preheat the oven to 180°C (350°F/gas mark 4).

4 Carefully peel away the skin, leaving the layer of white fat intact. Using a sharp knife, score the fat diagonally to make a diamond pattern.

5 Put the whiskey in a pan with the honey, redcurrant jelly, balsamic vinegar and ground allspice. Bring to the boil, then reduce the heat and simmer for 10 minutes, stirring occasionally, until slightly thickened. Stud the ham with the cloves and put in a large roasting tin with a little water to prevent the bottom from catching and burning. Brush a layer of the glaze all over the ham, reserving the remainder. Cook in the oven for 1 hour, brushing over another layer of the glaze every 15 minutes, until it's all gone. Transfer to a platter and leave to rest for 15–20 minutes before carving into slices to serve. Use as required.

Traditional Roast Goose with Honey & Clove Sauce

Traditionally, goose was the bird to eat at Christmas rather than turkey. Although turkey certainly leaves plenty for leftovers, for a smaller family gathering a roast goose is a special treat that's not to be missed. Just remember that you will need to order it in advance.

SERVES 6–8

1 x 4.5kg (10lb) oven-ready goose (use the giblets for the stock on page 78)

1 quantity stuffing (see pages 66, 69, 70 and 74 – potato is my favourite)

3 tbsp clear honey

For the honey and clove sauce:

225ml (8fl oz) goose stock (page 78) or beef stock

4 tbsp clear honey

2 tbsp light brown sugar

2 tbsp dark soy sauce

2 tbsp balsamic vinegar

2 tbsp tomato ketchup

2 tsp whole cloves

sea salt and freshly ground black pepper

1 Preheat the oven to 220°C (425°F/gas mark 7).

2 Remove any surplus fat from the cavity of the goose and spoon the stuffing loosely into the neck end, then fold over the skin and secure the underside with two skewers. Tie the bird in a neat shape with string, then sprinkle with salt and put on a large wire rack set in a roasting tin. Roast in the oven for 30 minutes.

3 Take the goose out of the oven and pour off any excess fat (which of course can be used for your roasties – see page 52). Reduce the oven temperature to 180°C (350°F/gas mark 4). Remove the wire rack and put the goose back in the tin and roast for another hour, again pouring off any excess fat after 30 minutes. Take the goose out of the oven and pour off any last excess fat, then brush all over with the honey. Roast for a final 30 minutes, until the juices run clear when the thickest part of the leg is pierced. A digital thermometer pushed into the breast should read 65–70°C (149–158°F). Transfer to a platter and leave to rest for 20 minutes, covered loosely with foil.

4 Meanwhile, to make the sauce, put all the ingredients in a small pan. Bring to the boil, then reduce the heat and simmer for 5 minutes, until thickened to a sauce consistency that coats the back of a spoon. Season and pass through a fine sieve into a clean pan to reheat gently.

5 Carve the goose, stirring any juices into the sauce. Put on warmed plates with some of the stuffing and spoon a little of the honey and clove sauce over.

Golden Crunch Roast Potatoes

While turkey may be the star of the Christmas table, if you get your roast potatoes right, then frankly you could serve chicken nuggets and most people would still be happy as Larry. Let's face it, we are all about the potatoes as a nation! This recipe also works for 900g (2lb) of parsnips – simply blanch for 3 minutes instead and cook for about 45 minutes. Try to use beef dripping for the best flavour. Check out James Whelan Butchers online for an award-winning dripping that can be delivered straight to your door.

SERVES 8–10

1.5kg (3¼lb) floury potatoes, such as Rooster, Desiree, King Edward or Maris Piper

4 tbsp beef dripping, goose or duck fat (from a jar or left over from a roast)

sea salt

handful of fresh rosemary sprigs (optional)

1 Preheat the oven to 190°C (375°F/gas mark 5).

2 Wash and peel the potatoes, reserving the peel. Cut the potatoes in half or into quarters, depending on their size. Put them in a large pan of salted boiling water along with the peel – it's easiest if you can put this in a muslin infusing bag. Parboil for 8 minutes.

3 Meanwhile, put the beef dripping, goose or duck fat in a large roasting tin and put it into the oven to heat. Drain the potatoes and discard the peel, then put them back in the pan and shake gently to rough up the edges. Take the roasting tin out of the oven and put on the hob over a gentle heat. Put the potatoes in one by one – they should sizzle as they hit the pan – and baste all over. Season with salt.

4 Roast in the oven for about 1 hour, until golden and crunchy, keeping an eye on them and basting with a little more fat if they begin to look dry. Add some fresh rosemary sprigs (if using) about 20 minutes before the end of the cooking time. Serve immediately, as these do not appreciate hanging around!

VARIATION

Roasted Potatoes with Truffle & Parmesan

For a really decadent twist, once the roast potatoes are cooked, sprinkle them with a couple teaspoons of your favourite truffle oil, then scatter over freshly grated Parmesan cheese to serve.

Perfect Mashed Potatoes

This is a brilliant mashed potato recipe, which once mastered can be adapted for different results. Try replacing a couple tablespoons of the milk with crème fraîche or cream for a richer version.

SERVES 8–10

1.5kg (3¼lb) floury potatoes, such as Rooster, peeled and cut into even-sized chunks

120ml (4fl oz) milk

75g (3oz) butter

sea salt and freshly ground black pepper

snipped fresh chives, to garnish

1 Put the potatoes in a large pan of salted water. Bring to the boil, cover and reduce the heat. Simmer for 15–20 minutes, until the potatoes are tender but aren't breaking up. Drain and return to the pan set over a low heat to dry out. Mash the potatoes or pass them through a potato ricer or vegetable mouli if you want a really smooth finish.

2 Heat the milk in a small pan or in the microwave. Using a wooden spoon, beat the butter into the potatoes until melted, then beat in the warm milk until you have a smooth, creamy mash. Season to taste with salt and pepper and serve at once garnished with snipped fresh chives.

VARIATIONS

Colcannon

Colcannon is traditionally made in Ireland with kale and was always served at Halloween with a lucky charm wrapped up and tucked in the centre for one person to find. Put a knob of the butter and a tablespoon of water in a pan with a tight-fitting lid over a high heat. Add 225g (8oz) of finely shredded cabbage or kale with two finely chopped spring onions and a pinch of salt. Cover, shake vigorously and cook for 1½ minutes. Shake again and cook for another 1½ minutes, until the cabbage or kale is tender but still crisp. Beat into the mashed potatoes with the warm milk.

Champ

Melt 75g (3oz) of butter in a sauté pan set over a medium heat and sauté a bunch of spring onions that have been finely chopped for 2–3 minutes, until tender. Beat into the mashed potatoes with the warm milk and season to taste.

All-in-one Baked Vegetables

These vegetables not only taste delicious, they are also the perfect accompaniment to your turkey or any roast. But the best part is that they can be prepared well in advance, leaving nothing to do last minute – expect, of course, remembering to pop them in the oven! The oven temperature is quite flexible, so simply put the parcel on the bottom shelf of your oven depending on what you are cooking and adjust the cooking time accordingly. They will keep warm in the unopened parcel, leaving you with one less thing to worry about.

SERVES 8–10

675g (1½lb) carrots

675g (1½lb) parsnips

4 celery sticks

1 small onion, very finely chopped

2 tsp fresh thyme leaves

50g (2oz) butter

sea salt and freshly ground black pepper

1 Preheat the oven to 180°C (350°F/gas mark 4).

2 Peel the carrots and parsnips and cut into even-sized batons. Cut the celery into similar-sized batons. Take a large double sheet of tin foil or parchment paper and pile the vegetable batons in the middle.

3 Scatter the onion and thyme over the vegetables and dot with the butter, then drizzle over about 4 tablespoons of water. Season to taste with salt and pepper, then fold in the sides of the parcel to enclose the veg by bringing up the sides, then folding over and twisting the edges.

4 Put the foil or parchment bag on a baking sheet and roast for 1 hour, until the vegetables are meltingly tender and slightly caramelised.

5 To serve, either open the baked vegetable parcel at the table or carefully pour the vegetables and all of their juices into a nice big warmed dish.

Braised Red Cabbage with Pomegranate

This is an ideal vegetable to prepare in advance and is excellent with turkey, ham or goose. It will keep for up to a week in the fridge covered with cling film in a non-metallic bowl. It also freezes very well – simply pop into medium-sized freezer bags and leave to thaw out before reheating gently, either on the hob or in a casserole dish with a lid in the oven.

SERVES 8–10

4 tbsp duck or goose fat (from a jar or left over from a roast) or 2 tbsp rapeseed oil

1 red cabbage, trimmed, cored and finely shredded

2 red onions, thinly sliced

1 large Bramley cooking apple, peeled, cored and grated

100g (4oz) dried cranberries

300ml (½ pint) red wine

300ml (½ pint) pomegranate juice

6 tbsp redcurrant jelly

4 tbsp red wine vinegar

1 tsp mixed spice

½ tsp ground cinnamon

½ tsp ground ginger

good pinch of ground cloves

sea salt and freshly ground black pepper

pomegranate seeds, to garnish (optional)

1 Melt the duck or goose fat in a very large heavy-based pan set over a medium heat, then tip in the red cabbage and onions. Sauté over a medium-high heat for about 5 minutes, until just beginning to soften.

2 Stir in the apple and cranberries, then add the red wine, pomegranate juice, redcurrant jelly, red wine vinegar and spices. Season to taste. Bring to the boil, stirring occasionally, then reduce the heat and simmer for about 1 hour, stirring every 20 minutes, until the cabbage is meltingly tender. Transfer to a warmed dish and garnish with pomegranate seeds (if using) to serve.

Celeriac & Sweet Potato Boulangère

This hassle-free dish is perfect for the Christmas table. The layered-up celeriac, sweet potatoes and onions absorb all the stock. It can be made in advance and left to cool completely before covering with cling film and storing in the fridge for up to three days before you want to use it. Reheat covered with tin foil in a preheated oven set to 180°C (350°F/gas mark 4) for 30 minutes, until piping hot.

SERVES 8–10

2 tbsp rapeseed oil, plus extra for greasing

3 onions, thinly sliced (on a mandolin is best)

3 garlic cloves, thinly sliced

2 tbsp roughly chopped fresh flat-leaf parsley

1 tbsp chopped fresh mixed herbs (use a mixture of sage, rosemary and thyme)

1kg (2¼lb) sweet potatoes, peeled and thinly sliced (on a mandolin is best)

1 large celeriac, peeled and thinly sliced (on a mandolin is best)

900ml (1½ pints) chicken or vegetable stock

50g (2oz) butter, diced

25g (1oz) stale white breadcrumbs (sourdough is best)

sea salt and freshly ground black pepper

1 Preheat the oven to 200°C (400°F/gas mark 6).

2 Heat the oil in a frying pan set over a medium heat, then sauté the onions, garlic and herbs for 10 minutes, until soft and lightly golden. Season to taste.

3 Layer the sweet potatoes in a large baking dish with the onions and celeriac. Season each layer as you go and finish with an attractive overlapping layer of the sweet potatoes. Pour over the stock and top with knobs of butter.

4 Rub some foil with oil and place it over the dish, oil side down, and seal tightly. Bake in the oven for 45 minutes, then remove the foil and press the potatoes down with a fish slice. Scatter over the breadcrumbs and bake for another 15–20 minutes, until golden. Serve at once or leave to cool completely before covering and storing in the fridge until needed.

Crispy Brussels Sprouts with Preserved Lemon & Parmesan

Add a deliciously different side dish to your Christmas dinner spread with these moreish Brussels sprouts. Shallow frying your sprouts like this gives them a whole new depth of flavour that's like the addictive crispy seaweed (basically cabbage) you get in Chinese restaurants. The knack is to sizzle them gently so that by the time the cut side is deep brown, the rest of the vegetable has wilted in the heat. Use only super fresh Brussels sprouts that literally snap when you break them off the stalks.

SERVES 6–8

500g (18oz) Brussels sprouts

3 tbsp rapeseed or sunflower oil

25g (1oz) butter, chilled and diced

pinch of sea salt

2 tbsp finely diced preserved lemon (shop-bought or see page 176)

3 tbsp freshly grated Parmesan cheese

1 Peel off the outer leaves from the Brussels sprouts, then slice each one in half.

2 Heat the oil in a large frying pan set over a medium heat. Put the sprouts in the pan, cut side down, and let them sizzle for 10 minutes without disturbing them. After 5 minutes, dot over the butter and allow it to sizzle and brown – the sprouts need to be really crispy and dark brown. If they are only lightly brown, carry on cooking them for another 5 minutes, then turn over and continue to cook for another few minutes, until just cooked through and tender when pierced with a small sharp knife.

3 Remove the sprouts from the heat and season with salt, then scatter over the preserved lemon and toss until evenly coated. Sprinkle over the Parmesan and toss again before tipping into a warmed serving dish. Serve at once.

Smashed Turnip with Caramelised Shallots

Turnip (also known as swede) goes well with almost anything, but particularly a roast. You can make this in advance and keep it covered in the fridge for up to three days, then just reheat in the microwave or gently in a pan or covered with tin foil in the oven.

SERVES 8–10

1 tbsp rapeseed oil

50g (2oz) butter

6 shallots, very thinly sliced

½ tsp fresh thyme leaves

good pinch of caster sugar

1kg (2¼lb) turnip, peeled and cut into 2.5cm (1in) chunks

sea salt and freshly ground black pepper

1 Heat the oil and a knob of the butter in a frying pan set over a low heat. Add the shallots and thyme and gently sauté for about 20 minutes, until softened and golden. Sprinkle over the sugar and cook for another 5–10 minutes, until lightly golden brown. Remove from the heat and set aside until needed.

2 Meanwhile, put the turnip in a steamer set above a pan of simmering water and season with salt. Cover and cook for about 10 minutes, until tender.

3 When the turnips are cooked, roughly mash them with the rest of the butter. Season to taste, adding plenty of black pepper, and stir in most of the shallot mixture. Transfer to a warm dish and garnish with the rest of the caramelised shallots to serve.

Braised Peas with Bacon

This is a great way of making frozen peas or petits pois more interesting. Keep a bag in the freezer for emergencies and you'll have a lovely vegetable side dish in no time at all. It does reheat well, but as it takes so little time to make, it's possibly worth doing just before serving, as the mint will discolour a little otherwise.

SERVES 8–10

1 tbsp rapeseed oil

4 rindless streaky bacon rashers, diced

2 leeks, trimmed and finely chopped

2 spring onions, trimmed and thinly sliced

2 garlic cloves, thinly sliced

100ml (3½fl oz) dry white wine

150ml (¼ pint) chicken or vegetable stock

450g (1lb) frozen garden peas or petits pois

25g (1oz) butter

1 tbsp roughly torn fresh mint leaves

sea salt and freshly ground black pepper

1 Heat the oil in a large pan set over a medium heat. Add the bacon and sauté for about 5 minutes, until crisp. Scoop out onto a plate lined with kitchen paper and set aside.

2 Tip the leeks into the pan along with the spring onions and garlic. Reduce the heat to low and cook for 5 minutes, until softened, tossing occasionally to ensure it cooks evenly. Pour in the wine and bring to a simmer.

3 Add the stock and peas or petit pois and simmer for 3 minutes. Return the bacon to the pan with the butter and mint and season to taste. Allow to just heat through, then serve immediately in a warmed dish.

**

STUFFINGS, SIDES & SAUCES

**

Prunes & Sausages Wrapped in Bacon

This is an accompaniment that we tend to have with our turkey and the cocktail sausages are always a hit with the children. Try to buy good-quality dry-cured streaky bacon rashers, as they will hold their shape better and crisp up nicely.

SERVES 10–12

10 rindless dry-cured streaky bacon rashers (smoked or unsmoked)

20 cocktail sausages (about 450g (1lb))

10 ready-to-eat pitted prunes (about 150g (5oz))

1 Preheat the oven to 190°C (375°F/gas mark 5).

2 Stretch each bacon rasher with the back of a knife, then cut each rasher into three. Wrap a piece of bacon tightly around each cocktail sausage and prune, then put into a small roasting tin ready to cook, or you could cook them around the turkey. Either way, cook in the oven for 30 minutes, until the cocktail sausages are cooked through and the bacon is crisp. Serve hot arranged around the turkey or in a separate warmed dish.

Sausage Stuffing Roll with Dried Cranberries

Everyone has their favourite part of the Christmas meal, but for many it's the stuffing. The practical shape of this clever roll means it takes up very little space in the oven, as it can be slid in alongside a larger roasting tin. However, it can also be used to stuff the bird. Whatever you decide to do with it, it can be prepared up to three days in advance as long as the sausages are nice and fresh, meaning all you need to do on the big day is remember to pop it into the oven.

SERVES 10–12

100g (4oz) butter

1 onion, finely chopped

300g (11oz) good-quality sausagemeat

175g (6oz) fresh white breadcrumbs

50g (2oz) dried cranberries

1 tbsp chopped fresh flat-leaf parsley

2 tsp chopped fresh mixed herbs (use a mixture of sage, rosemary and thyme)

sea salt and freshly ground black pepper

1 Preheat the oven to 200°C (400°F/gas mark 6).

2 Melt the butter in a sauté pan set over a medium heat, then add the onion and sauté for about 5 minutes, until softened. Remove the pan from the heat and mix in the sausagemeat, breadcrumbs, dried cranberries and herbs, then season generously.

3 Shape into a large roll, then wrap in a layer of parchment paper and tin foil, twisting the ends securely to seal. Cook in the oven for about 45 minutes, until cooked through and tender. Unwrap just before cutting into slices to serve.

Apricot & Sage Stuffing Balls

This stuffing is very versatile and can also be cooked inside the bird or in a separate buttered dish so it becomes very crisp. It's really good with turkey, goose or even chicken. These can be made two or three days in advance and kept in the fridge until needed.

MAKES 9

75g (3oz) butter, plus extra for greasing

1 large onion, diced

1 tbsp chopped fresh sage

175g (6oz) fresh white breadcrumbs

100g (4oz) dried apricots, finely chopped

finely grated rind of 1 small orange

1 tbsp chopped fresh flat-leaf parsley

sea salt and freshly ground black pepper

1 Melt the butter in a frying pan set over a medium heat, then add the onion and sage and cook for a few minutes, until the onion has softened but not coloured. Put the breadcrumbs in a bowl and tip in the onion mixture, then mix well to combine and season to taste. Fold in the apricots, orange rind and parsley. Roll into nine balls and either arrange around the bird or place in a small buttered roasting tin.

2 When ready to cook, preheat the oven to 180°C (350°F/gas mark 4).

3 Cook the stuffing balls in the oven for about 20 minutes, until cooked through and golden brown. Serve immediately in a warmed dish.

Irish Potato Stuffing

This traditional Irish recipe complements goose perfectly. The sharpness of the apples helps to counteract the richness of the goose. However, it would also be delicious with turkey, whether cooked inside the bird or alongside in a buttered ovenproof dish.

MAKES ENOUGH TO STUFF 1 X 4.5KG (10LB) OVEN-READY GOOSE OR TURKEY ....

900g (2lb) floury potatoes, such as Rooster, scrubbed but not peeled

40g (1½oz) butter, plus extra for greasing and to serve if cooking in a dish

2 onions, finely chopped

1 large Bramley cooking apple, peeled, cored and diced

2 tbsp chopped fresh flat-leaf parsley

2 tsp chopped fresh thyme

sea salt and freshly ground black pepper

1 Season the potatoes with salt and steam over a pan of simmering water for 30–40 minutes, until completely tender. Remove from the heat and put a clean tea towel on top to soak up the excess moisture, then leave for another 5 minutes. Once the potatoes are cool enough to handle, peel off the skins and then mash until smooth.

2 Melt half the butter in a pan set over a low heat, then add the onions and sauté for 10 minutes, until softened but not coloured. Add the apple and continue to cook until it breaks down into a fluff. Beat in the rest of the butter, then fold into the warm mashed potatoes with the herbs and season to taste. Leave to cool completely. This can be stored for up to two days covered with cling film in the fridge.

3 When ready to cook, preheat the oven to 180°C (350°F/gas mark 4).

4 Butter an ovenproof dish and spoon in the potato stuffing. Bake in the oven for 30–35 minutes, until golden brown, and serve straight to the table dotted with a few small knobs of butter. Alternatively, use to fill the cavity of the goose and cook as per the instructions for roasting the goose on page 48.

Christmas Herb & Onion Stuffing

This is a really good recipe for the buttery fresh herb stuffing that everyone seems to love and I have been making it for years, ever since watching my mother Vera making it as a young child. If you prefer it can be cooked and served in a separate dish (rather than in the bird itself), which makes it more crispy and golden. However, I tend to use it to stuff the cavity and neck of the bird so that it soaks up all the delicious juices while cooking.

MAKES ENOUGH TO STUFF 1 X 4.5–5.4KG (10–12LB) TURKEY

175g (6oz) butter

2 onions, finely chopped

500g (18oz) fresh white breadcrumbs

25g (1oz) fresh flat-leaf parsley sprigs, leaves finely chopped

15g (½oz) fresh thyme sprigs, leaves only

15g (½oz) fresh rosemary sprigs, leaves finely chopped

sea salt and freshly ground black pepper

1 Melt the butter in a frying pan set over a low heat, then add the onions and sauté for about 10 minutes, until softened but not coloured. Tip into a bowl and mix in the breadcrumbs and herbs, then season generously. Leave to cool completely.

2 Use the stuffing to three-quarters fill the cavity of the bird, then secure the flaps of skin over the cavity with a metal skewer. Use the rest of the stuffing to fill the crop of the neck end. Start at the neck end, where you'll find a flap of loose skin. Gently loosen this away from the breast and you'll be able to make a triangular pocket. Pack the stuffing inside as far as you can go and make a neat round shape on the outside, then tuck the neck flap underneath the bird and secure it with a small skewer. Cook as per the instructions for roasting the turkey on page 38.

VARIATION
Fruity Chestnut & Sage Stuffing

If you would like to ring in the changes, try adding 200g (7oz) of chopped canned or vacuum-packed chestnuts to the stuffing along with a couple handfuls of dried cranberries or chopped dried apricots. This version also benefits from the addition of a good tablespoon of chopped fresh sage and even a small packet of toasted pine nuts for a different texture.

Perfect Christmas Gravy

A good gravy is a crucial component to the Christmas meal and many a dinner is judged on its success. It really is worth making a good stock with the giblets for the best flavour. If you haven't got Madeira, use port or red wine instead. If you want to get ahead, make the gravy the day before using butter instead of the fat, then add it to the roasting tin and bring to a simmer for a few minutes, stirring constantly.

MAKES ABOUT 500ML (18 FL OZ)

1 heaped tbsp plain flour

3 tbsp Madeira

600ml (1 pint) turkey or goose stock (page 78)

1 tbsp redcurrant jelly (optional)

sea salt and freshly ground black pepper

1 Pour the turkey or goose juices from the roasting tin into a jug, then spoon off 2 tablespoons of the fat (which will be floating on the top) and put this back into the unwashed tin. Spoon off any remaining fat from the cooking juices and discard.

2 Put the roasting tin directly on the hob over a gentle heat and stir the flour into the residue in the tin. Cook on the hob for a minute or two, stirring, until golden. Pour in the Madeira, stirring to combine, then gradually add the stock, stirring until smooth after each addition. Bring to the boil and let it bubble for about 10 minutes, until reduced and thickened, stirring occasionally.

3 Whisk in the redcurrant jelly (if using) until dissolved, then add the skimmed juices from the roasted bird back into the gravy and season to taste. Strain into a warmed gravy boat to serve.

Turkey or Goose Stock

Ask your butcher for the giblets with your bird of choice, as they make excellent stock. I always soak mine in cold water overnight to remove any impurities. If you like a richer stock, roast the giblets in a small roasting tin in a preheated oven set to 200°C (400°F/gas mark 6) for about 15 minutes, until lightly browned, before using them.

MAKES ABOUT 600ML (1 PINT)

giblets from the turkey or goose (neck, heart and gizzard but not the liver)

1 onion, quartered (not peeled)

1 carrot, roughly chopped

1 celery stick, roughly chopped

6 black peppercorns

2 bay leaves

1 sprig of fresh thyme

small handful of parsley stalks

Put the giblets into a large pan. Add 1 litre (1¾ pints) of cold water and bring to the boil, skimming off any scum that rises to the surface. Add the remaining ingredients, then reduce the heat and simmer gently for 1 hour. Strain the stock into a jug and leave to cool completely. Cover with cling film and chill for up to a day before using as required.

Creamy Bread Sauce

Once made, this will keep covered in the fridge for up to five days. You can also freeze this after the second step of the method for up to one month. Defrost in the fridge for 24 hours, then complete the recipe.

MAKES ABOUT 900ML (1½ PINTS)

1 large onion, quartered

8 whole cloves

800ml (1 pint 7fl oz) milk

10 black peppercorns

4 bay leaves

175g (6oz) fresh white breadcrumbs

40g (1½oz) butter

4 tbsp cream

a little freshly grated nutmeg

sea salt and freshly ground black pepper

1 Stud each onion quarter with the cloves. Put into a pan with the milk, peppercorns and three of the bay leaves. Put over a low heat and slowly bring to simmering point. Remove from the heat and set aside for 1 hour to allow the flavours to develop.

2 Strain the milk into a clean pan. Stir in the breadcrumbs and butter and simmer over a medium heat for a few minutes, stirring, until thickened. Stir in the cream and bring back to simmering point, then season to taste. (The sauce can be frozen at this point.)

3 Transfer to a warmed gravy boat. Garnish with the remaining bay leaf and sprinkle with a little nutmeg to serve.

Cranberry Sauce

This simple cranberry sauce is so much nicer than anything you can buy. It's delicious with roast turkey as well as any type of game or cold cuts on St Stephens Day.

MAKES ABOUT 450ML (¾ PINT)

350(12oz) fresh or frozen cranberries

175g (6oz) granulated sugar

Put the cranberries in a pan with 4 tablespoons of water. Bring to the boil, then cover the pan, reduce the heat and simmer for 6–8 minutes, until the cranberries have started to soften. Stir in the sugar until dissolved, then remove from the heat. Serve warm or cold in a serving dish. This can be kept covered with cling film in the fridge for up to a week.

Cranberry Relish

Once made, this will keep covered in the fridge for up to one week. If you want to make it in advance, leave it to cool and freeze in a food bag for up to one month.

MAKES ABOUT 600ML (1 PINT)

25g (1oz) butter

1 small onion, finely sliced

½ tsp chopped fresh rosemary

120ml (4fl oz) ruby red port

500g (18oz) fresh or frozen cranberries

200g (7oz) light brown sugar

Melt the butter in a pan set over a medium heat. Add the onion and rosemary and cook for 5 minutes to soften. Pour in the port and allow it to bubble down. Add the cranberries and simmer for 8–10 minutes, until the cranberries have softened. Stir in the sugar until it has dissolved. Transfer to a serving bowl and serve at room temperature.

Cranberry Salsa

This is tangy and sweet with a bit of a bite to serve with leftover turkey dishes, particularly of the Mexican variety, or even with some tortilla chips to use as a dip.

350g (12oz) fresh cranberries

150g (5oz) caster sugar

1 Granny Smith apple, peeled, cored and chopped

1 small red onion, chopped

1 small red pepper, cored and chopped

1 mild fresh green chilli, deseeded and chopped

juice of 1 lime

4 tbsp chopped fresh coriander

sea salt and freshly ground black pepper

Put all the ingredients in a food processor and pulse until just combined but still with some texture. Transfer to a bowl and season to taste, then cover with cling film. Set aside for at least 2 hours to allow the flavours to develop (or up to a week in the fridge is fine). Use as required.

MacNean Frangipane Mince Pies with Brandy Butter

These can be made up to three days in advance or frozen and refreshed in a moderate oven set at 180°C (350°F/gas mark 4) for 8–10 minutes before glazing.

MAKES 18

For the brandy butter:
150g (5oz) icing sugar, sifted
100g (4oz) butter, softened
3 tbsp brandy (preferably Cognac)

For the pastry:
175g (6oz) plain flour, plus extra for dusting
100g (4oz) cold butter, diced
50g (2oz) caster sugar
1 egg yolk, plus beaten egg to glaze
½ tbsp cream
½ tsp lemon juice

For the frangipane:
100g (4oz) butter
100g (4oz) caster sugar
2 large eggs
100g (4oz) ground almonds
1 tbsp plain flour
1 tbsp dark rum
1 vanilla pod, split in half lengthways and seeds scraped out

For the filling and topping:
1 x 400g (14oz) jar of mincemeat
25g (1oz) flaked almonds
apricot jam, to glaze
icing sugar, for dusting

1 To make the brandy butter, cream together the icing sugar and butter. Beat in 1 tablespoon of boiling water and the brandy until smooth. Put in a dish, cover and chill until needed.

2 To make the pastry, put the flour, butter and caster sugar in a food processor and blend for 20 seconds. Add the egg yolk, cream and lemon juice and blend just until the pastry comes together. Wrap in cling film and chill for 1 hour.

3 Preheat the oven to 200°C (400°F/gas mark 6).

4 To make the frangipane, put the butter and caster sugar in a large bowl. Using a hand-held mixer, beat until soft and creamy. Scrape down the sides, then add the eggs and continue to beat. Add the ground almonds, flour, rum and vanilla seeds and mix briefly.

5 Roll the pastry out thinly on a lightly floured work surface and cut into 18 x 6.5cm (2½in) circles and use these to line the bun tins. Spoon a teaspoon of mincemeat into each tartlet and top with the frangipane. There is no need to spread the mixture flat, as it will level out in the oven (but don't overfill the tins). Sprinkle a few flaked almonds on top of each one. Bake in the oven for 15–17 minutes, until cooked through and light golden, watching carefully. Remove the mince pies from the tins and allow to cool a little on a wire rack.

6 Dilute the apricot jam with a little water and bring to the boil, then brush the top of each warm tartlet with this glaze. These are best served warm with a light dusting of icing sugar.

Auntie Maureen's Plum Pudding

In my opinion, no one makes Christmas pudding as good as my Auntie Maureen! Its flavour only improves as time goes on, so it's best to make it a month before you plan to eat it. Serve warm or cold with lashings of custard or whipped cream with and brandy butter.

MAKES 2 X 1.2 LITRE (2 PINT) PUDDINGS

50g (2oz) plain flour

½ tsp ground mixed spice

½ tsp ground cloves

¼ tsp ground nutmeg

225g (8oz) sultanas

175g (6oz) butter, melted, plus extra for greasing

175g (6oz) fresh white breadcrumbs

175g (6oz) light brown sugar

175g (6oz) raisins

50g (2oz) currants

50g (2oz) candied mixed peel

50g (2oz) blanched almonds, chopped

½ apple, peeled, cored and diced

½ small carrot, grated

finely grated rind and juice of 1 lemon

2 eggs, lightly beaten

300ml (½ pint) stout

icing sugar, to decorate (optional)

custard or whipped cream, to serve

brandy butter (page 86), to serve

1 Sift together the flour, mixed spice, cloves and nutmeg in a large bowl. Add the sultanas, melted butter, breadcrumbs, sugar, raisins, currants, mixed peel, almonds, apple, carrot and the lemon rind and juice and mix until well combined. Gradually add the beaten eggs, stirring constantly, followed by the stout. Mix everything thoroughly and cover with a clean tea towel, then leave in a cool place overnight.

2 Use the fruit mixture to fill 2 x 1.2 litre (2 pint) greased pudding bowls. Cover with a double thickness of greaseproof paper and tin foil, then tie tightly under the rim with string.

3 To cook, preheat the oven to 150°C (300°F/gas mark 2).

4 Stand each pudding basin in a large cake tin three-quarters full of boiling water, then cook in the oven for 6–8 hours (or you can steam them for 6 hours in the usual way). Cool and re-cover with clean greaseproof paper. Once cooked, the plum pudding can be stored in a cool, dry place for up to two months.

5 On Christmas Day, re-cover with greaseproof paper and foil. Steam for 2–3 hours, until completely cooked through and tender. Decorate with a light dusting of icing sugar, if liked.

6 To serve, cut the plum pudding into slices and arrange on serving plates. Have a separate jug of the custard or a dish of whipped cream and another of brandy butter so that everyone can help themselves.

Vera's Sherry Trifle

This is one dessert that I can clearly remember from my childhood – it probably even enticed me to be a chef. My mum always made this for special occasions and I just loved helping, especially with the cleaning of the bowls... Now I like to decorate the top with pomegranate seeds to make it sparkle like jewels.

SERVES 6

200g (7oz) Madeira cake, broken into pieces

300ml (½ pint) cream

toasted flaked almonds, to decorate

pomegranate seeds, to decorate

spun sugar, to decorate (optional)

For the custard:

300ml (½ pint) milk

100ml (3½fl oz) cream

½ vanilla pod, split in half lengthways and seeds scraped out

5 egg yolks

4 tbsp caster sugar

2 tsp cornflour

For the fruit:

100ml (3½fl oz) sweet sherry

100g (4oz) caster sugar

½ vanilla pod, split in half lengthways and seeds scraped out

1 x 500g (18oz) bag of frozen fruits of the forest

1 To make the custard, put the milk, cream and vanilla pod and seeds in a heavy-based pan set over a gentle heat and cook until it nearly reaches the boil – but don't allow to boil. Meanwhile, put the egg yolks, sugar and cornflour in a large bowl and whisk together until pale and thickened.

2 Remove the hot milk and cream mixture from the heat and slowly whisk it into the egg mixture through a fine sieve until smooth. Discard the vanilla pod and pour back into the pan, then set over a gentle heat. Cook, without allowing it to boil, until the custard coats the back of a wooden spoon, stirring continuously. Remove from the heat and leave to cool, covered with a piece of cling film pressed directly on the surface of the custard to prevent a skin from forming on top.

3 Meanwhile, prepare the fruit. Put the sherry in a large pan with the sugar and vanilla seeds and bring to the boil. Reduce the heat and simmer for 4–5 minutes, until syrupy, stirring occasionally. Stir in the frozen fruits of the forest and set aside until cooled, stirring occasionally. The fruits should defrost naturally in the hot syrup but still hold their shape.

4 Scatter the Madeira cake over the base of a 1.5 litre (2½ pint) glass serving bowl. Spoon over the fruit and cover with the cooled custard. Chill for 1 hour, until the custard sets a little firmer, or up to 24 hours is fine.

5 When ready to serve, whip the cream in a bowl until you have achieved soft peaks. Put spoonfuls on top of the custard, then gently spread with a palette knife or the back of a spoon to cover the custard completely (or you can use a piping bag). Sprinkle over the toasted flaked almonds and pomagranate seeds and decorate with some spun sugar if liked, then place straight on the table to serve.

Rocky Road Christmas Tower

This is a great recipe to make with children – it's just hard to stop them from eating it before it goes into a tin! The finished bars can also be cut into bite-sized pieces if you prefer and would make a lovely present wrapped in tissue paper in a nice box.

MAKES 1 TOWER (ABOUT 24 BARS)

2 x 58g (2oz) Mars bars

300g (11oz) plain or milk chocolate, broken into squares

75g (3oz) butter

2 tbsp pouring golden syrup

125g (4½oz) rich tea biscuits, broken up into small pieces

100g (4oz) mini marshmallows

40g (1½oz) Maltesers

1 Chop up the Mars bars into small pieces and put in a pan with the chocolate, butter and golden syrup. Cook over a low heat for 3–4 minutes, until melted, then beat until smooth. Leave to cool a little.

2 Fold the rich tea biscuits into the Mars bar mixture with the mini marshmallows and Maltesers until well combined. Transfer to a 17.5cm (7in) shallow square tin that has been lined with non-stick baking paper and spread out evenly with a spatula. Place in the fridge for at least 4 hours (or overnight is best) to set.

3 Cut into bars and arrange on a cake stand stacked up to look like a tower. These will keep well in a rigid plastic container with a lid for up to a week in the fridge and are handy to have tucked away as treats over the festive season.

Gingerbread House

This recipe makes a perfectly crisp gingerbread house that will have everyone gasping in delight. The smell of the biscuits baking in the oven will instantly transport you to Christmas heaven!

MAKES 1 GINGERBREAD HOUSE

225g (8oz) butter

200g (7oz) light brown sugar

4 tbsp golden syrup

2 tsp treacle

2 tbsp ground ginger

2 tbsp ground cinnamon

½ tsp ground cloves

500g (18oz) plain flour

1 tsp bicarbonate of soda

To decorate:

1 egg white

250g (9oz) icing sugar, plus extra for dusting

a few drops of lemon juice

1 x 125g (4½oz) packet of mini chocolate fingers

generous selection of different kinds of sweets

1   Preheat the oven to 190°C (375°F/gas mark 5). Cut out the templates (see page 97).

2   Put the butter, sugar, golden syrup, treacle, ginger, cinnamon and cloves in a pan set over a low heat. Cook for 3–4 minutes, stirring, to melt the butter and dissolve the sugar. Remove from the heat and stir in the flour and bicarbonate of soda in batches until you have a smooth but fairly stiff dough. Be careful, as the dough will be quite hot. Allow it to cool for about 5 minutes before handling. However, it's important to work with the dough while it's still a little warm and pliable, as it becomes quite dry and crumbly once it has cooled completely, making it more difficult although not impossible to work with.

3   Roll out a quarter of the dough in between two large sheets of parchment paper to a 3mm (⅛in) thickness – basically, as thin as you can because you want the gingerbread to rise only slightly so it will be nice and crisp when it's cool. Cut out one of the sections, then slide the gingerbread, still on its parchment paper, onto a baking sheet. Repeat with the remaining dough, re-rolling the trimmings, until you have two side walls, a front and back wall, two roof panels and a base. Any leftover dough can be cut into Christmas trees, if you like.

4   Bake all the sections in the oven for 10–12 minutes, until firm and just a little darker at the edges. Leave to cool for a few minutes to firm up, then trim them again to give sharp edges. Leave to cool.

5   Put the egg white in a large bowl, then sift in the icing sugar, add the lemon juice and stir to make a thick, smooth icing. Spoon into a piping bag fitted with a medium nozzle. Pipe generous snakes of icing along the wall edges, one by one, to join the walls together. Use a small bowl to support the walls from the inside, then allow to dry for at least a couple of hours.

6 Once dry, remove the supports and fix the roof panels on. The angle is steep, so you may need to hold these on firmly for a few minutes, until the icing starts to dry. Leave to dry completely (overnight is best).

7 To decorate, pipe a little icing on the mini chocolate fingers, cutting them down to fit as necessary.

8 Using the icing, stick sweets around the door and on the front of the house. Use any remaining icing to decorate the house. Pipe a little icing around the top. If you've made gingerbread trees, decorate those too. Dust the roof with icing sugar for a snowy effect. Lay a winding path of sweets and fix gingerbread trees around and about using blobs of icing. Your gingerbread house will be edible for about a week but will last a lot longer if you just want to use it for decorative effect.

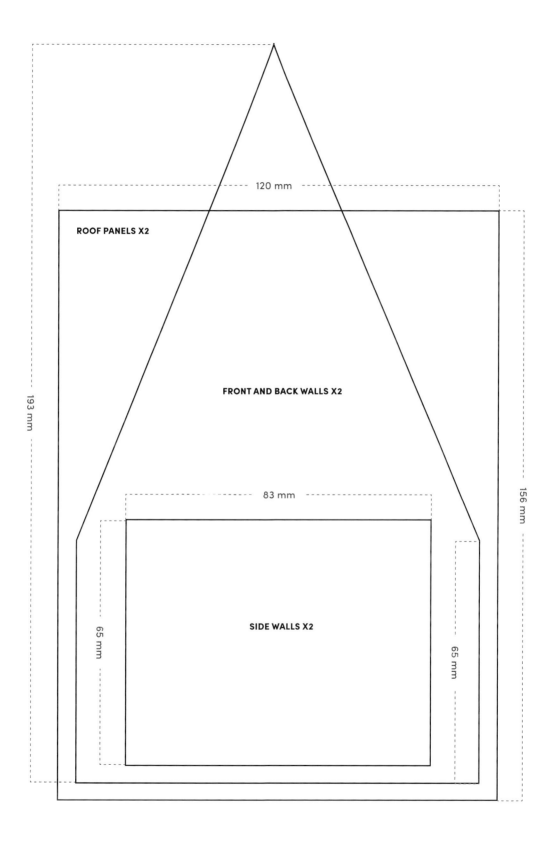

ROOF PANELS X2

FRONT AND BACK WALLS X2

SIDE WALLS X2

120 mm

193 mm

156 mm

83 mm

65 mm

65 mm

Eccles Cakes

I recently came across a version of an Eccles cake that was a flaky pastry filled with currants and immediately fell in love. This is my version, which I think goes exceptionally well with a wedge of mature Cheddar cheese. They can also be baked from frozen for unexpected guests who you want to impress.

MAKES 8

500g (18oz) all-butter puff pastry, thawed if frozen

plain flour, for dusting

For the filling:
175g (6oz) mixed dried fruit
50g (2oz) mixed peel
4 tbsp light brown sugar
1 tbsp melted butter
½ tsp ground cinnamon
½ tsp ground ginger
finely grated rind of 1 orange

For the glaze:
1 egg, lightly beaten
1 tbsp Demerara sugar
½ tsp ground cinnamon

1 Roll out the puff pastry on a lightly floured work surface until it's 5mm (¼in) thick – it needs to be just big enough to stamp out 8 x 10cm (4in) rounds, which you can easily check with the cutter. Once you are happy that it's big enough, using a 10cm (4in) cutter, stamp out eight puff pastry rounds. Arrange them on a baking sheet and pop into the fridge to rest for at least 10 minutes while you make the filling.

2 Put the dried fruit in a bowl and stir in the mixed peel, sugar, melted butter, spices and orange rind. Get the pastry from the fridge and put a tablespoonful of the mixture into the centre of each round, then gather the pastry around the filling to enclose and squeeze it together. Flip them over and gently pat them into a smooth round. Flatten each round a little more with the palm of your hand into an oval approximately 7.5cm x 6cm (3in x 2¼in). Put them in the fridge on a baking sheet lined with non-stick baking paper for 10 minutes to firm up.

3 Preheat the oven to 200°C (400°F/gas mark 6).

4 Once the Eccles cakes have rested, use a small sharp knife to make three little slashes in the top of each one. Brush with the beaten egg to glaze, then mix together the Demerara sugar and cinnamon and sprinkle on top.

5 Bake in the oven for 15–20 minutes, until the pastry is puffed up and golden brown. Remove from the oven and leave to cool for 5 minutes before eating.

Yule Log

This delightful French bûche de Noêl always goes down a treat. As it's so rich you'll find a little goes a long way, so make the slices small. This also happens to be gluten free if you use gluten-free chocolate.

SERVES 8–10

butter, for greasing

100g (4oz) plain chocolate (at least 70% cocoa solids), broken into squares

4 large eggs, separated

100g (4oz) caster sugar, plus extra for dusting

For the icing:

225g (8oz) butter, softened

200g (7oz) icing sugar, sifted, plus extra to decorate

2 tbsp good-quality cocoa powder, sifted

1 tbsp vanilla extract

1 Preheat the oven to 190°C (375°F/gas mark 5). Butter a 33cm x 23cm (13in x 9in) Swiss roll tin, line with non-stick baking paper and butter the paper.

2 Melt the chocolate in a heatproof bowl set over a pan of simmering water, making sure the water doesn't touch the bottom of the bowl.

3 Whisk the egg yolks with the caster sugar until very thick and pale in colour. Beat in the egg whites until stiff, then fold into the melted chocolate. Transfer into the prepared tin and spread out evenly. Bake in the oven for 20–25 minutes, until risen and firm to the touch.

4 Turn the sponge out onto a sheet of greaseproof paper generously sprinkled with caster sugar. Carefully peel off the lining paper. Cover the roulade with a warm damp tea towel and leave to cool.

5 To make the icing, use an electric hand-held mixer to whisk the butter and icing sugar in a large bowl until light and fluffy. Add the cocoa powder and vanilla and whisk until you have a smooth icing. Spread one-third of the icing over the cold roulade. Using the paper to help, roll up the roulade to enclose the filling.

6 Put the filled roulade on a long plate or board and trim down the edges at an angle, then use these pieces to make a 'branch' coming off to the side. Spread the Yule log with the rest of the icing, covering the whole thing completely so that it looks like a big log with a branch coming off the side. Using a skewer, create a wood-like texture on the icing.

7 To serve, transfer the roulade onto a serving plate and dust generously with icing sugar, then cut into slices.

PART 3

***

THE
HOLIDAY
SEASON

***

***

BREAKFASTS & BRUNCHES

***

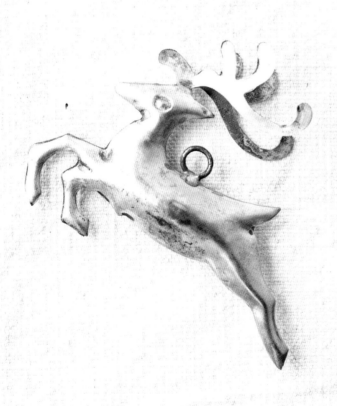

One-tray Full Irish

It's lovely to treat everyone to a leisurely breakfast over the festive season, but the clearing up can spoil the pleasure. This version not only cooks everything together in the oven, but it can be brought straight to the table with a flourish! If you've got the time, a trip to the nearest farmers market should get you everything you need.

SERVES 6–8

8 large butcher-style sausages

8 flat chestnut mushrooms, stems trimmed

4 ripe plum tomatoes, cut in half

rapeseed oil, for drizzling

½ tsp fresh thyme leaves

4 large slices of black pudding, such as McCarthy's of Kanturk, halved

8 large eggs

8 rindless dry-cured bacon rashers

1 large batch loaf, cut into slices

butter, softened, for spreading (try Cuinneog's Farmhouse Country Butter)

sea salt and freshly ground black pepper

freshly brewed tea, to serve

Dalkey Mustard, to serve

Ballymaloe Relish, to serve

1 Preheat the oven to 200°C (400°F/gas mark 6).

2 Put the sausages in a large, sturdy, non-stick roasting tin and bake in the oven for 10 minutes. Remove the tin from the oven and give the sausages a good shake – this will help to distribute any fat that is now in the pan. Add the mushrooms and tomatoes and drizzle with a little rapeseed oil, then sprinkle over the thyme and season to taste. Return to the oven for another 10 minutes.

3 Remove the roasting tin from the oven and tuck in the pieces of black pudding, then quickly break in the eggs and add the rashers. Put back in the oven and cook for 6–8 minutes, until the eggs are cooked to your liking and the rashers have begun to crisp up around the edges.

4 Meanwhile, make your toast and butter it and put a large pot of tea on to brew. To serve, put the roasting tin straight on the table and allow everyone to help themselves. Have small bowls of mustard and relish to hand around separately.

Pecan & Maple Crumble Muffins

There's something special about waking up to the smell of muffins wafting around the house. To get ahead you can have the crumble made and covered in the fridge and the dry ingredients in a bowl ready to go so that it won't take you much more than 5 minutes to get them into the oven.

MAKES 12 MUFFINS

For the crumble:
50g (2oz) plain flour
40g (1½oz) butter, chilled and cut into cubes
40g (1½oz) light brown sugar
½ tsp ground cinnamon
pinch of sea salt

For the muffins:
275g (10oz) self-raising flour
100g (4oz) pecan nuts, roughly chopped
75g (3oz) light brown sugar
1 tsp bicarbonate of soda
small pinch of sea salt
175ml (6fl oz) buttermilk
120ml (4fl oz) sunflower oil
50ml (2fl oz) maple syrup
2 large eggs

1 Preheat the oven to 180°C (350°F/gas mark 4). Line a muffin tin with 12 paper cases.

2 First make the crumble topping. Put all the ingredients in a mini blender or food processor and pulse it for about 15 seconds, until the mixture resembles breadcrumbs.

3 To make the muffins, put the flour, pecans, sugar, bicarbonate of soda and salt in a bowl and mix to combine. Mix the buttermilk, sunflower oil, maple syrup and eggs in a jug, then pour into the dry ingredients. Mix together using as few stirs as possible for lighter, fluffier muffins.

4 Using a large spoon or ice cream scoop, divide the mixture between the paper cases, using a spatula to ensure you get every last bit out of the bowl. Sprinkle over an even layer of the crumble topping.

5 Bake in the oven for 18–20 minutes, until the muffins are cooked through. To test, a skewer inserted into the centre of a muffin should come out nice and clean. Once cooked, remove from the oven and allow to cool a little in the tin. These muffins are best served warm or at least on the day that they are made.

Cinnamon Swirl Pancakes with Cream Cheese Glaze

These delicious cinnamon swirl pancakes need no syrup, as they are drizzled with a cream cheese glaze instead. They're actually quite filling and you might find that one is enough for breakfast, perhaps with some fresh fruit alongside. Try them with blackberries and blueberries or slices of banana would also work well.

MAKES 6–8 PANCAKES

For the cream cheese glaze:

100g (4oz) unsalted butter

50g (2oz) soft cream cheese, at room temperature

100g (4oz) icing sugar, sifted

½ tsp vanilla extract

For the pancakes:

250g (9oz) plain flour

large pinch of sea salt

2 large eggs, lightly beaten

400ml (14fl oz) buttermilk

1 heaped tsp ground cinnamon

sunflower oil, for frying

To serve:

fresh blackberries

fresh blueberries

1 To make the glaze, melt the butter in a pan set over a low heat. Remove from the heat and whisk in the cream cheese until almost smooth. Tip in the icing sugar and vanilla extract and whisk again until smooth. Set aside while you make the pancakes.

2 Put the flour and a pinch of salt in a bowl and make a slight dip in the middle with a fork. Break in the eggs and add a little of the buttermilk, then beat until smooth, adding enough of the rest of the buttermilk to make a smooth, thick batter.

3 Remove 100ml (3½fl oz) of the batter and mix the cinnamon into it, then place in a squeezy bottle or a ziplock bag that you can snip the corner off of.

4 Heat a medium non-stick frying pan over a medium heat. Using kitchen paper, smear the pan with a little oil, then spoon in large spoonfuls of the batter – each pancake should be approximately 10cm (4in) in diameter. You'll need to cook the pancakes in batches.

5 Reduce the heat to low. Snip off one corner of the ziplock bag with the cinnamon batter, if using, and make a swirl in each pancake. You'll need to work quickly and leave a border around the edge of each pancake so the swirl doesn't spill over.

6 Once bubbles begin to appear on the pancakes, turn them over using a wide metal spatula and cook for another 2–3 minutes, until golden. Keep warm on a plate while you cook the remainder, wiping the pan with oiled kitchen paper after each batch.

7 When ready to serve, reheat the cream cheese glaze over a low heat. Arrange the pancakes on warmed plates with fresh blackberries and blueberries and drizzle over the cream cheese glaze.

Grilled Streaky Bacon with Smashed Avocado on Toast & Poached Egg

This moreish combination of creamy avocado and crispy bacon on toast topped off with a runny poached egg is well worth getting up for. If you want to get ahead, the poached eggs can be kept in a bowl of cold water in the fridge for up to two days, then simply slipped into a pan of boiling water to reheat as needed. Tomatoes take on an intensely deep flavour after roasting and can be used in so many different ways, but are particularly good as part of a relaxed breakfast over the holidays. They will also keep for a couple of days covered with cling film in the fridge and can be brought back up to room temperature before using.

SERVES 4

8 dry-cured streaky bacon rashers

1 tbsp white wine vinegar

4 large eggs

4 thick slices of white crusty loaf or sourdough bread

a little extra virgin olive oil

2 firm, ripe avocados, halved and stoned

½ lemon

fresh micro herbs, to garnish

For the roasted tomatoes:

4 vine-ripened tomatoes, halved

2 garlic cloves, sliced

1 sprig of fresh thyme

2 tbsp extra virgin olive oil

1 tbsp balsamic vinegar

sea salt and freshly ground black pepper

1   Preheat the oven to 150°C (300°F/gas mark 2).

2   Arrange the tomatoes on a baking tray and scatter over the garlic and thyme leaves. Drizzle over the extra virgin olive oil and balsamic vinegar and season generously. Roast for 1 hour, then leave to cool before using.

3   Preheat the grill to a medium heat. Grill the bacon rashers until crisp and golden brown on both sides, then drain well on kitchen paper.

4   Fill a large saucepan with water. Add the vinegar and a pinch of salt and bring to a hard boil over a high heat. Once boiling, reduce the heat so the water is simmering, then use a spoon to swirl the water into a whirlpool. Crack in the eggs one at a time and cook for 2½ minutes, then drain well on kitchen paper.

5   Toast the bread in a toaster or on the griddle and drizzle with a little olive oil, then arrange on warmed plates. Scoop the avocados into a bowl, mash with a squeeze of lemon and season to taste. Divide between the toast, top with two crispy bacon rashers and put a poached egg on each slice. Season with a final pinch of sea salt and a grinding of black pepper. Serve with two roasted tomato halves alongside and scatter over micro-herbs.

MacNean Eggs Benedict with Spinach

This is a variation on classic eggs Benedict, a perfect breakfast dish. If you're going to be short of time in the morning, prepare the poached eggs up to two days before you need them, as they will sit perfectly happily in the fridge in a bowl of cold water. Omit the ham for a great vegetarian option and serve with some roasted tomatoes instead (see page 111).

SERVES 4

1 tbsp white wine vinegar

4 large eggs

40g (1½oz) unsalted butter, softened

350g (12oz) baby spinach leaves

2 white muffins, split in half

225g (8oz) hand-carved cooked ham, trimmed

For the chive cream sauce:

50ml (2fl oz) cream

1 tsp Dijon mustard

1 tsp softened butter

1 tsp snipped fresh chives

sea salt and freshly ground black pepper

1 Heat a large pan with 2.25 litres (4 pints) of water. Add the white wine vinegar with a pinch of salt and bring to the boil. Break each egg into the water where it's bubbling, then move the pan to the edge of the heat and simmer gently for 2½ minutes. Remove the poached eggs with a slotted spoon and plunge into a bowl of iced water. When cold, trim down any ragged ends from the cooked egg white. These will keep happily in the fridge for up to two days in a bowl of cold water.

2 When ready to serve, preheat the grill.

3 Add half of the butter to a large pan set over a fairly high heat. Once it starts to foam, tip in the spinach and sauté until just wilted. Season to taste and drain off any excess liquid. Keep warm.

4 Arrange the muffin halves on a grill pan, cut side up, and cook for 2–3 minutes, until lightly toasted. Spread with the remaining butter.

5 Meanwhile, bring a large pan of salted water to the boil. Add the poached eggs and cook for 1 minute to warm them through.

6 To make the sauce, put the cream and mustard in a small pan and simmer for 1 minute. Whisk in the butter and stir in the chives. Season to taste and keep warm.

7 To serve, put the muffins on warmed plates and arrange the ham on top, then spoon on small mounds of the drained spinach. Using a slotted spoon, remove the poached eggs from the pan and drain briefly on kitchen paper. Place on top of the spinach and spoon over the chive cream sauce.

Porridge Bread with Scrambled Eggs & Smoked Salmon

This is a great breakfast if you have a large crowd to feed and don't want to spend the whole morning doing it! The bread has great keeping properties and can happily be made the day before. Otherwise it literally takes 5 minutes to make and is also good toasted for up to three days. Use the carton of yogurt to measure out the porridge oats and once you've made it, save a clean carton for the next time. If you prefer your scrambled eggs more chunky, don't whisk the egg and cream mixture – pour or break the eggs straight into the pan and then add the cream, stirring continuously.

SERVES 8

450g (1lb) smoked salmon, cut into slices or ribbons

For the porridge bread:

1 x 500g (18oz) tub of natural yogurt

1 large egg

2 tbsp olive oil

2 x 500g (18oz) cartons of porridge oats

2 tsp bicarbonate of soda

1 tsp salt

handful of oat bran (optional)

For the scrambled eggs:

12 eggs

6 tbsp milk

1 tbsp snipped fresh chives, plus extra whole ones to garnish

75g (3oz) butter, softened

sea salt and freshly ground black pepper

1 Preheat the oven to 200°C (400°F/gas mark 6). Lightly oil a 900g (2lb) loaf tin.

2 Put the yogurt, egg and olive oil in a bowl and mix to combine, then mix in the porridge oats, bicarbonate of soda, salt and oat bran (if using). Tip into the oiled tin, then even out the top by pressing down lightly with a fork. Bake in the oven for 45 minutes, until golden brown, then turn out of the tin and carefully put back in the oven directly on the oven shelf for another 5–10 minutes to dry out the crust. Leave to cool on a wire rack.

3 When almost ready to serve, whisk together the eggs, milk, chives and plenty of freshly ground black pepper. Heat a knob of the butter in a non-stick frying pan set over a low to medium heat. Once the butter is foaming, add the egg mixture and whisk continuously for 2–3 minutes, until just set but still soft. Remove from the heat, as the eggs will continue to cook, and gently fold in the smoked salmon. Check the seasoning and add a pinch of salt if you think it needs it.

4 Meanwhile, cut the porridge bread into slices and spread each one with a little butter. Arrange on warmed plates. Add the scrambled eggs and garnish with the whole chives to serve.

One-tray Spinach & Gruyère Brunch

This American-inspired recipe is very similar to a savoury bread and butter pudding that can be made and left to soak overnight so that all you need to do is pop it into the oven in the morning. It really is quite filling but would be fantastic with some roasted tomatoes (see page 111), which can also be made in advance. Alternatively, add slices of ham and perhaps a smear of mustard to the sandwiches or simply serve with some leftover ham.

SERVES 4—6

50g (2oz) butter, softened, plus extra for greasing

5 shallots, minced

550g (1¼lb) spinach, tough stalks removed and washed

8 slices of multigrain brown bread (or similar)

175g (6oz) Gruyère cheese, finely grated

6 large eggs

5 tbsp milk

sea salt and freshly ground black pepper

1 Melt a knob of the butter in a sauté pan set over a medium heat. Add the shallots and sauté for about 5 minutes, until softened but not coloured. Stir in the spinach in fistfuls and sauté until just softened and wilted. Season to taste and drain in a colander and then on kitchen paper to remove all the excess moisture.

2 Use the rest of the butter to spread on the slices of bread, then fill with the cooled spinach mixture and sprinkle over half of the cheese. Cut each sandwich in half to make two triangles, then arrange in a buttered ovenproof dish that is 27cm x 21cm (10½in x 8¼in) and 6cm (2¼in) deep.

3 Break the eggs into a bowl and add the milk, then season generously and whisk until just combined. Pour over the sandwiches that are tightly packed in the dish and press down gently with a fish slice to ensure they are all soaked evenly. Cover with cling film and put in the fridge overnight or you can cook it immediately if you prefer, but if you've got the time, try to give it at least half an hour for the bread to soak up all of the liquid.

4 Preheat the oven to 200°C (400°F/gas mark 6).

5 Remove the cling film and sprinkle over the remaining cheese. Bake in the oven for 25 minutes, until just golden brown. Serve at once straight to the table.

***

ST STEPHEN'S DAY
& LEFTOVERS

***

Fragrant Turkey Lettuce Cups with Satay Dressing

This is my kind of salad when you're looking for something easy to rustle up from what you've got left in the fridge. It should take no more than 20 minutes to get on the table, particularly if you use a mandolin for the vegetables, and is full of fresh, spicy flavours that should perk up those taste buds.

SERVES 4–6

For the dressing:

3 tbsp peanut butter

2 tbsp sunflower oil

2 tbsp Chinese chilli bean sauce (or substitute with black bean or sriracha sauce)

1 tbsp caster sugar

1 tbsp dark soy sauce

2 tsp rice wine vinegar

1 tsp balsamic vinegar

For the salad:

2 Little Gem lettuces

1 carrot, cut into julienne

¼ cucumber, halved, deseeded and cut into julienne

2 spring onions, trimmed and shredded

15g (½oz) fresh coriander, leaves chopped

handful of fresh mint leaves, chopped

juice of 1 lime

500g (18oz) cooked turkey, removed from the bone

2 tsp toasted sesame seeds

1 To make the dressing, put the peanut butter in a bowl and whisk in 2 tablespoons of boiling water, then add the rest of the ingredients and continue to whisk until you have achieved a thick dressing. Set aside at room temperature until needed.

2 Separate the Little Gem lettuces into leaves, discarding any outer damaged leaves. Arrange on a large platter.

3 Put the carrot, cucumber and spring onions in a bowl. Add the coriander, mint and lime juice, then toss until evenly combined. Add a small mound of this salad to each lettuce leaf.

4 Remove any skin from the turkey and finely shred the flesh. Place on top of the crunchy vegetable mixture and drizzle the peanut dressing on top. Garnish with the sesame seeds to serve.

Turkey & Ham Pie with Puff Pastry

If you're a fan of wanting to eat a second Christmas dinner to make the best of your leftovers, then this is the pie for you. The sauce takes a little bit of time to make, but the end result is so worth it that there might even be a discussion about which was the best dinner! Serve with some stuffing on the side if you're lucky enough to have any left and a bowl of mashed potatoes.

SERVES 6–8

75g (3oz) butter

1 large onion, finely chopped

2 carrots, diced

2 celery sticks, diced

2 tsp fresh thyme leaves

50g (2oz) plain flour, plus extra for dusting

350ml (12fl oz) chicken or turkey stock (page 78) or use up any leftover gravy

120ml (4fl oz) dry white wine

2 small leeks, trimmed and thinly sliced

100g (4oz) button mushrooms, halved

150ml (¼ pint) cream

2 tsp Dijon mustard

450g (1lb) leftover cooked turkey, cut into bite-sized pieces

275g (10oz) leftover cooked ham, cut into bite-sized pieces

500g (18oz) all-butter puff pastry, thawed if frozen

egg wash, to glaze (1 egg or yolk beaten with a splash of milk)

sea salt and freshly ground black pepper

1 Heat 25g (1oz) of the butter in a large sauté pan set over a medium heat. Add the onion, carrots, celery and thyme and sauté for 6–8 minutes, until tender but not coloured. Add the rest of the butter and allow to melt, then stir in the flour and cook for 1 minute. Whisk in the stock and/or gravy and the wine until the sauce is thickened and smooth.

2 Bring to a simmer, then add the leeks and mushrooms and cook for 3–4 minutes, until tender. Stir in the cream and mustard and cook for another minute or two, stirring. Season to taste, then remove from the heat and fold in the turkey and ham. Transfer to a 25cm (10in) pie dish (or use a large ovenproof dish if you don't have one). Leave to cool.

3 Preheat the oven to 180°C (350°F/gas mark 4).

4 Roll out the puff pastry on a lightly floured board until it's the thickness of a €1 coin and large enough to easily cover the pie dish. Brush the edge of the pie dish with egg wash, then cover with the pastry. Use a sharp knife to trim down as necessary and use a fork to lightly press around the edge to crimp it. Stamp or cut out leaves from the pastry leftovers and use to decorate the pie if liked. Brush with more egg wash and make a small hole in the middle to allow the steam to escape.

5 Bake in the oven for about 40 minutes, until the pastry is cooked through and golden brown. Serve straight to the table.

Parmesan Risotto

One of the beautiful things about risotto is that it's a blank canvas in terms of both flavour and appearance. It can be adorned with toppings with an array of crunchy and creamy textures, which will give the finished dish more complex flavours.

SERVES 4

1.5 litres (2½ pints) chicken or turkey stock (page 78)

2 tbsp olive oil

50g (2oz) butter, diced

1 small onion, finely chopped

1 garlic clove, finely chopped

1 tsp fresh thyme leaves

350g (12oz) Carnaroli rice (risotto rice)

150ml (¼ pint) dry white wine

5 tbsp freshly grated Parmesan

sea salt and freshly ground black pepper

1 Pour the stock into a pan and bring up to a gentle simmer. Heat the oil and a knob of the butter in a separate large pan. Add the onion, garlic and thyme and cook over a medium heat for 4–5 minutes, until softened but not coloured, stirring occasionally.

2 Increase the heat and add the rice. Cook for 1 minute, stirring continuously, until all the grains are evenly coated and the rice is opaque. Pour in the wine and allow it to reduce for 1–2 minutes, stirring. Reduce the heat to medium, then add a ladleful of the warm stock and allow it to reduce down, stirring until it has been completely absorbed into the rice.

3 Continue to add the simmering stock a ladleful at a time, stirring frequently. Allow each addition of stock to be almost completely absorbed before adding the next ladleful. Cook until the rice is al dente – just tender but with a slight bite. This should take 20–25 minutes.

4 Just before serving, stir in the remaining butter with the Parmesan and season to taste. Ladle into warmed bowls to serve.

VARIATIONS

Ham & Petits Pois with Blue Cheese

When you're adding the last ladleful of stock, tip in 225g (8oz) of leftover cooked diced ham with a couple handfuls of frozen petits pois. Crumble some blue cheese on top and garnish with fresh thyme and finely grated lemon rind just before serving.

Seafood

Use mascarpone instead of Parmesan and add any leftover seafood you've got to hand, such as prawns or shrimp, lobster, crab or smoked salmon. Finish with chopped fresh flat-leaf parsley.

Turkey & Wild Mushrooms

Soak a packet of dried porcini mushrooms in hot water. Add the reconstituted mushrooms with the rice, using the soaking water instead of some of the stock. Fold in 225g (8oz) of cooked diced turkey along with some sautéed garlicky mushrooms.

One-pot Harissa Turkey & Butternut Squash Curry

This clever curry is quick and tasty and uses harissa paste for its kick and is a lovely way of using up the Christmas leftovers, but you could also use a tablespoon of your favourite curry powder or paste instead. If you prefer a smooth sauce, then simply blend with a stick blender before adding the butternut squash, which could be replaced with regular or sweet potatoes.

SERVES 4–6

1 tbsp rapeseed oil

1 large onion, finely chopped

2 garlic cloves, finely chopped

2.5cm (1in) piece of fresh ginger, peeled and grated

1 tsp ground turmeric

4–6 tbsp harissa paste (chilled from a carton)

250ml (9fl oz) Greek-style yogurt

1 x 400g (14oz) tin of chopped plum tomatoes

300ml (½ pint) vegetable stock

1 butternut squash, peeled, seeds removed and cut into cubes

4–6 large handfuls of leftover turkey, chopped into bite-sized pieces

2 large handfuls of baby spinach leaves

toasted flaked almonds, to garnish

dried cranberries, to garnish

fresh micro coriander sprigs, to garnish

Mediterranean wraps, to serve

tzatziki (shop-bought or homemade), to serve

1 Heat the oil in a large pan set over a medium heat. Add the onion and cook for 2–3 minutes, then add the garlic, ginger and turmeric and cook for another minute or so.

2 Stir in the harissa paste to taste, then add the yogurt one large spoonful at a time, stirring continuously. Add the tomatoes and stock, then stir in the butternut squash. Cover with a lid and cook gently for 25–35 minutes, until the butternut squash is tender.

3 Stir in the turkey and spinach leaves and allow to just warm through. Garnish with the flaked almonds, dried cranberries and micro coriander sprigs and serve with the wraps and tzatziki.

Festive Couscous Salad with Pomegranate & Pistachio Nuts

If you don't fancy using all turkey, replace some of the amount with chunks of feta or a mild crumbled goats' cheese. It would also be delicious with a drizzle of pomegranate molasses just before serving if you happen to have some lurking in your cupboard.

SERVES 6–8

350g (12oz) couscous

juice of 2 lemons

6 tbsp extra virgin olive oil

900ml (1½ pints) chicken stock

100g (4oz) raw shelled pistachio nuts

450g (1lb) cooked turkey and/or ham, shredded

100g (4oz) dried cranberries

50g (2oz) chilli mixed seeds

4 tbsp chopped fresh flat-leaf parsley

handful of fresh mint leaves, torn

75g (3oz) pomegranate seeds

sea salt and freshly ground black pepper

1 Put the couscous in a heatproof bowl and add the lemon juice and half of the oil, stirring to ensure all the grains are well coated. Heat the stock in a pan and season to taste, then pour it over the couscous, cover tightly with cling film and set aside for about 10 minutes, until all the liquid has been absorbed.

2 Meanwhile, lightly toast the pistachio nuts in a dry heavy-based frying pan set over a low heat for about 5 minutes, then remove from the heat and roughly chop.

3 Stir the remaining 3 tablespoons of oil into the couscous with the toasted nuts, turkey and/or ham, dried cranberries, chilli mixed seeds and herbs. Season to taste. Scatter over the pomegranate seeds to serve.

Christmas Coleslaw with Turkey & Ham

Leave out the turkey and ham and you've got the most delicious winter coleslaw you've ever tasted. It would be perfect to serve to a vegetarian with cold cuts on the side for anyone who fancied meat. This is guaranteed to liven up any gathering and is ideal to make in advance and it travel wells if you're bringing a dish to someone's house.

SERVES 8–10

100g (4oz) pecan nuts

2 tbsp softened butter

2 tbsp light brown sugar

½ tsp dried chilli flakes

1 small Savoy cabbage, outer leaves discarded or used in another dish

1 small red cabbage, trimmed, cored and finely shredded

1 large firm, ripe mango, peeled, finely diced and stone discarded

1 mild fresh red chilli, deseeded and finely sliced

15g (½oz) fresh mint, leaves torn

15g (½oz) fresh coriander, leaves roughly chopped

225g (8oz) leftover cooked turkey, shredded

175g (6oz) leftover cooked ham, shredded

sea salt and freshly ground black pepper

For the dressing:

juice of 3 limes

1 lemongrass stalk, finely chopped

3 tbsp maple syrup

1 tsp dark soy sauce

¼ tsp dried chilli flakes

4 tbsp extra virgin rapeseed oil

2 tbsp toasted sesame oil

1 First make the dressing. Put the lime juice in a small pan with the lemongrass, maple syrup, soy sauce and chilli flakes and reduce over a high heat for a few minutes, until thick and syrupy. Remove from the heat and allow to cool, then strain into a bowl to remove the lemongrass pieces. Whisk in the rapeseed and toasted sesame oil to form a thick emulsion. Set aside until needed.

2 To caramelise the pecans, put them in a frying pan and dry roast for a few minutes over a medium–high heat, stirring occasionally, until they are nicely toasted. Add the butter, tossing to coat as soon as it has melted. Sprinkle over the sugar and chilli flakes with a good pinch of salt. Continue to toss the nuts in the pan as the sugar caramelises. Tip them out onto a sheet of non-stick baking paper, quickly spread them out and leave to cool completely, then roughly chop.

3 Mix the Savoy and red cabbage in a large bowl with the dressing. Fold in the mango and chilli with the herbs. Finally, fold in the turkey and ham with the caramelised nuts and season to taste. Spread out on a large platter to serve.

Turkey Quesadillas with Mango Salsa

There are so many ways of using up the turkey and/or ham leftovers, but none as simple as quesadillas. They should be ready to eat in just 5 minutes and are always a hit with children, who might prefer them with cherry tomatoes instead of the mango salsa. If you are making a large number of them they can also be baked in the oven with good success.

MAKES 2

¼ red onion, thinly sliced

4 soft flour tortillas

1 mild fresh red chilli, cut into rings (optional)

225g (8oz) leftover cooked turkey, sliced (or use ham or a mixture of both)

2 handfuls of grated red Cheddar and mozzarella

For the mango salsa:

1 firm, ripe mango, peeled, finely diced and stone discarded

1 small roasted red pepper, peeled, deseeded and diced

finely grated rind and juice of 1 lime

2 tbsp chopped fresh basil

2 tbsp sweet chilli sauce

1 tbsp rapeseed oil

sea salt and freshly ground black pepper

1 First make the mango salsa. Put all the ingredients in a bowl and mix to combine, then season to taste. Cover with cling film and set aside at room temperature to allow the flavours to develop.

2 Scatter the red onion on two of the tortillas and sprinkle over the chilli (if using). Arrange the slices of turkey or ham (or a mixture of both) on top, then cover with the cheese and remaining tortillas.

3 Heat a large non-stick frying pan over a medium heat. Add the quesadillas one at a time and cook for about 2 minutes on each side, until lightly toasted. Cut into wedges and serve with mango salsa on the side.

VARIATION

Christmas Quesadillas with Brie & Cranberry

The obvious time for this one is after Christmas, when there is plenty of turkey about. If you have leftover stuffing, substitute some slices of stuffing for some of the turkey and/or ham. Scatter slices of Brie or Camembert over the turkey and/or ham, add small dollops of cranberry sauce and sprinkle over some toasted pine nuts. Season generously and scatter over a little watercress. Cook as described above.

***

NEW YEAR & ENTERTAINING

***

Instant Tomato Soup with Bacon & Cheese Scones

This soup is a great way to get excellent flavour using the best tins of whole peeled Italian tomatoes that you can find in the supermarket or deli.

SERVES 6–8

2 tbsp rapeseed oil

1 large onion, finely chopped

2 x 400g (14oz) tins of whole Italian peeled tomatoes

good pinch of caster sugar

300ml (½ pint) chicken or vegetable stock (from a cube is fine)

200ml (7fl oz) cream

For the scones:

200g (7oz) bacon or pancetta cubes

splash of rapeseed oil

350g (12oz) self-raising flour, plus extra for dusting

1 tsp baking powder

1 tsp English mustard powder

75g (3oz) butter, well chilled and diced

150g (5oz) mature Cheddar cheese, grated

15g (½oz) fresh chives, finely sliced or snipped

1 heaped tbsp fresh thyme leaves

175ml (6fl oz) buttermilk

1 small egg beaten with a little buttermilk, to glaze

sea salt and freshly ground black pepper

1 Preheat the oven to 220°C (425°F/gas mark 7). Lightly dust a baking sheet with flour.

2 To make the scones, put the bacon or pancetta in a frying pan with a splash of oil and cook over a medium heat until crispy, then tip out onto kitchen paper to drain.

3 Put the flour, baking powder, mustard and a pinch of salt in a bowl. Rub in the butter until it looks like fine breadcrumbs. Stir in the cooked bacon, cheese and herbs, then make a well in the centre and add the buttermilk. Stir with a round-bladed knife to make a soft dough, then bring together to form a ball.

4 Roll out the dough on a lightly floured surface to a 3cm (1¼in) thickness. Using an 8cm (3¼in) fluted square cutter, stamp out the scones (or you could just use a knife to cut them into squares). Put on the floured baking sheet and brush with the egg wash. Bake in the oven for 10–12 minutes, until risen and golden brown.

5 Meanwhile, make the soup. Heat the oil in a large pan set over a medium heat. Add the onion and gently sauté for 5 minutes, until softened. Using your hands, crush in the tomatoes, then season and add the sugar. Stir in the stock, cover and simmer for 5 minutes. Stir in the cream and blitz until smooth with a hand-held blender. Reheat gently and ladle into bowls to serve with the scones on the side.

Potted Poached Salmon with Sourdough Toasts

This starter looks like you've been slaving away all day in the kitchen when it actually takes only minutes to make. It uses poached salmon, which is a fantastic product to have on stand-by over the festive season.

SERVES 8–12

1 x 180g (6¼oz) tub of full-fat cream cheese

4 tbsp crème fraîche or sour cream

1 tbsp creamed horseradish

500g (18oz) shop-bought poached salmon fillet, all skin and bones removed

2 sprigs of fresh dill, finely chopped

15g (½oz) fresh chives, finely chopped

juice of ½ lemon

sea salt and freshly ground black pepper

slices of toasted sourdough or white baguette, to serve

lambs lettuce, to serve

quartered radishes, to serve

sliced gherkins, to serve

1 Mash the cream cheese in a large bowl with the crème fraîche or sour cream and horseradish. Flake in the poached salmon, then add the dill, chives and lemon juice. Season with salt and pepper and gently fold together until evenly combined. Spoon the salmon into jars or ramekins. This can be served straight away or left overnight to chill, either sealed or covered tightly with cling film.

2 Serve on a platter with slices of toasted sourdough or white baguette, lambs lettuce, radishes and gherkins.

Fragrant Slow Roast Leg of Lamb with Mediterranean Salad

This leg of lamb is fragrantly spiced before being baked for nearly 5 hours, until its flesh is almost soft enough to part from its bones with a spoon – yum!

SERVES 6–8

4 large garlic cloves

finely grated rind of 1 lemon

2 tbsp chopped fresh rosemary

2 tbsp chopped fresh thyme

2 tsp ground cumin

½ tsp sweet paprika

4 tbsp extra virgin olive oil

1 x 2.3kg (5lb) leg of lamb

juice of 2 lemons

1kg (2¼lb) waxy potatoes, such as Nicola, halved

minty yogurt, to serve

For the salad:

3 tbsp extra virgin olive oil

2 tsp red wine vinegar

1 small red onion, very thinly sliced

½ cucumber, halved lengthways, deseeded and thinly sliced

225g (8oz) mixed cherry tomatoes, halved

150g (5oz) baby spinach leaves

75g (3oz) black Kalamata olives, stoned and quartered

15g (½oz) fresh flat-leaf parsley, leaves stripped and roughly chopped

sea salt and freshly ground black pepper

1 Crush the garlic, lemon rind and 1 teaspoon of salt in a pestle and mortar. Add the herbs, cumin, paprika and some black pepper and blend to a smooth pulp. Stir in 2 tablespoons of the olive oil. Using a sharp knife, make holes all over the lamb, then rub in the paste, pushing it into the holes. Transfer the lamb to a shallow dish (or a turkey bag) and add the lemon juice. Chill overnight to marinate.

2 The next day, take the lamb out of the fridge about 1 hour before you want to cook it. Preheat the oven to 160°C (325°F/gas mark 3).

3 Lay two long pieces of parchment paper on top of two long pieces of foil to form a cross. Tip in the potatoes, toss in the remaining 2 tablespoons of oil and season to taste. Bring up the sides of the foil to create a pile of the potatoes, then pour over the marinade from the lamb. Sit the lamb on top of the potatoes and seal the foil to enclose. Put into a roasting tin and roast in the oven for 4½ hours, until the lamb is meltingly tender.

4 Remove the lamb from the oven and increase the temperature to 220°C (425°F/gas mark 7). Unwrap the parcel and scrunch the tin foil and paper under the rim of the tin, then baste the lamb and return to the oven for 20 minutes, until browned. Put the lamb on a platter, wrap it in the foil and set aside to rest. Turn the potatoes and return them to the oven for 30 minutes, then season with salt.

5 Meanwhile, make the salad. Use the oil and vinegar to dress the rest of the ingredients in a bowl. Shred the lamb from the bone and arrange on warmed plates with the potatoes and salad. Add spoonfuls of mint yogurt to serve.

Aromatic Crusted Butterflied Lamb with Caramelised Garlic & Orange Salsa

This marinade is a version of bulgogi from Korea that is absolutely delicious with lamb, particularly if you leave it to marinate for a couple of days.

SERVES 6–8

1 x 3kg (6½lb) leg of lamb, boned and well trimmed (butterflied), roughly 5cm (2in) thick

1 bunch of spring onions, trimmed and roughly chopped

5cm (2in) piece of fresh root ginger, peeled and chopped

3 tbsp dark soy sauce

2 tbsp dry sherry

2 tbsp toasted sesame seeds

1 tbsp toasted sesame oil

1 tsp black peppercorns

½ tsp light brown sugar

For the salsa:

3 tbsp olive oil

1 garlic clove, finely chopped

1 fresh red chilli, deseeded and finely chopped, plus extra to garnish

4 tsp caster sugar

2 tsp balsamic vinegar

1 small orange

15g (½oz) fresh mint, leaves stripped and shredded, plus extra to garnish

1 tbsp lemon juice

sea salt and freshly ground black pepper

1 Put the lamb in a shallow dish (or use a turkey bag if you have one). Put the rest of the ingredients in a food processor and blend to a thick paste, then rub it all over the lamb. Cover with cling film and chill for up to two days to marinate.

2 Preheat the oven to 230°C (450°F/gas mark 8).

3 Bring the lamb back up to room temperature. Put on a rack in a roasting tin, cut side up, and season well. Roast in the oven for 20 minutes, then turn over and roast for 15 minutes for rare. If you prefer your lamb more well done, cook it for an extra 15–20 minutes.

4 Meanwhile, make the salsa. Heat the olive oil in a pan set over a medium-high heat. Add the garlic and chilli and cook for 1–2 minutes, until lightly golden, stirring occasionally. Add 3 teaspoons of the sugar along with the balsamic vinegar, a good pinch of salt and 6 tablespoons of water. Bring to the boil, then reduce the heat and simmer for 3–5 minutes, until most of the liquid has evaporated and the garlic and chilli are covered with a thick syrup.

5 Pare the rind from the orange, avoiding the white pith, cut into 1mm julienne and put into a small pan. Squeeze the juice from the orange and make up to 100ml (3½fl oz) with water. Pour this over the julienned rind and add the remaining teaspoon of sugar. Bring to a simmer over a medium heat and cook for 6–8 minutes, until the liquid has reduced by about one-third. Remove from the heat. Stir the mint and lemon juice into the caramelised garlic with enough of the julienned orange rind mixture to sweeten. Put in a bowl and season to taste.

6 Remove the lamb from the oven and rest in a warm place for 10 minutes. If you don't like your lamb too pink, cover it with foil and it will continue to cook. Carve into slices and add any of the cooking juices to the salsa. Arrange the lamb on warmed plates with the salsa and garnish with mint leaves to serve.

Twice-baked Goats' Cheese Soufflés with Pear & Walnut Salad

These can be made ahead of time and will puff up again when you put them back in the oven, leaving very little to do last minute.

SERVES 6

350ml (12fl oz) milk

1 small onion, cut in half

1 bay leaf

3 black peppercorns

40g (1½oz) butter, plus extra for greasing

40g (1½oz) self-raising flour, plus extra for dusting

3 large eggs, separated

200g (7oz) hard goats' cheese, such as Knockdrinna, rind removed and cheese grated

micro herbs, to garnish

For the salad:

50g (2oz) walnut halves

2 firm, ripe pears

juice of 1 lemon

2 tbsp extra virgin olive oil

sea salt and freshly ground black pepper

1 Preheat the oven to 180°C (350°F/gas mark 4). Grease and lightly flour 6 x 200ml (7fl oz) ramekins.

2 Pour the milk into a pan set over a low heat, then add the onion, bay and peppercorns. Bring to a simmer, then strain into a jug.

3 Melt the butter in a clean pan, then add the flour, whisking to combine. Slowly add the warm milk, whisking continuously until you have a thick white sauce. Simmer gently for 2–3 minutes. Transfer to a large bowl and whisk in the egg yolks and three-quarters of the grated cheese. Beat the egg whites in a separate bowl until they are light and fluffy and forming soft peaks, then fold into the mixture.

4 Divide the mixture between the ramekins and put them in a bain-marie (a roasting tin half-filled with just-boiled water). Bake in the oven for 15 minutes, until well risen and lightly golden. Allow to cool, then cover with cling film and chill for up to 24 hours.

5 To finish the soufflés, remove them from the fridge and preheat the oven to 180°C (350°F/gas mark 4). Sprinkle the rest of the cheese on top and return to the oven for about 5 minutes, until heated through and they have puffed back up.

6 Meanwhile, make the pear salad. Put the walnuts on a baking tray and toast in the oven for 8–10 minutes, until lightly golden. Leave to cool a little, then roughly chop. Using a mandolin or very sharp knife, cut the pear into wafer-thin slices and toss them in the lemon juice.

7 To serve, add a small mound of the pear and walnut salad on the side of each plate and drizzle with the extra virgin olive oil. Put a soufflé, still in its ramekin, in the centre of each plate and add a grinding of black pepper, then scatter over the walnuts and garnish with the micro herbs.

Roast Rib of Beef on the Bone with Port & Cashel Blue Gravy

A rib of beef is perfect when you've got a crowd to feed. Try to start with a piece of beef that has been hung for 21 days for the best flavour and texture and always let it come back up to room temperature before roasting.

SERVES 6–8

1 tsp black peppercorns

1 tbsp English mustard powder

1.5kg (3¼lb) French-trimmed rib of beef on the bone, at room temperature

3 tbsp rapeseed oil

2 large onions, peeled and quartered with root left intact

2 large carrots, halved lengthways

1 garlic bulb, cut in half

small handful of soft thyme leaves, plus extra to garnish

2 tsp plain flour

4 tbsp ruby red port

400ml (14fl oz) beef or chicken stock

75g (3oz) Cashel Blue cheese, rind removed and cheese crumbled into small pieces

sea salt and freshly ground black pepper

creamed horseradish, to serve

1 Preheat the oven to 230°C (450°F/gas mark 8).

2 Toast the peppercorns in a dry frying pan until aromatic, then put in a pestle and mortar and grind until cracked. Mix in the mustard and 2 teaspoons of salt. Wipe the meat with damp kitchen paper and rub with the mustard mix.

3 Heat 1 tablespoon of the oil in a frying pan that's large enough to take the rib of beef. Add the beef and quickly sear until lightly browned on all sides.

4 Pour the rest of the oil into a roasting tin, then add the onions, carrots, garlic halves and thyme, tossing to coat. Season to taste, then sit the seared beef in the middle of the vegetables. Roast in the oven for 15 minutes, then reduce the oven temperature to 200°C (400°F/gas mark 6) and roast for 10 minutes per 450g (1lb) for rare, 12 minutes for medium-rare and 20–25 minutes for well done. A joint this size will take just under 1 hour to cook to medium-rare. Take out and baste halfway through the cooking time.

5 When the beef is cooked to your liking, transfer to a platter with the garlic halves, cover with tin foil and leave to rest for 30 minutes while you make the gravy.

6 Pour the juices from the roasting tin into a jug and leave the fat to settle on top, then skim off and discard. Put the roasting tin on the hob and stir in the flour, scraping the bottom of the tin with a wooden spoon to remove any residue. Gradually stir in the port and allow to bubble down completely. Pour in the stock and reserved juices and simmer for 10 minutes, stirring, until reduced by one-third. Strain into a clean pan, then whisk in the Cashel Blue until it has melted. Season with pepper and pour into a gravy boat.

7 To serve, carve the rested beef into slices and arrange on warmed plates with the roasted garlic and a dollop of creamed horseradish and garnish with extra sprigs of fresh thyme. Hand round the gravy separately.

Oriental Sticky Duck Breasts with Figs

This is a fantastic way of serving duck breasts, as there is very little preparation involved. They are best served slightly pink in the centre, but just cook them for a bit longer if you prefer them more well done.

SERVES 4–6

4–6 x 175g (6oz) Peking duck breasts, such as Thornhill

1 fresh red chilli, deseeded and finely chopped

4 tbsp kecap manis (sweet soy sauce)

2 tbsp clear honey

2 tbsp balsamic vinegar

pinch of salt

1 tsp Chinese five-spice powder

4–6 firm, ripe figs, sliced in half

steamed fragrant rice sprinkled with toasted sesame seeds, to serve

1 Trim down the fat from each duck breast to give a nice neat shape, then score the skin in a diagonal diamond pattern with a sharp knife. Put the chilli, kecap manis, honey and balsamic vinegar into a shallow dish (or use a large ziplock bag). Add the duck and leave to marinate in the fridge overnight or up to two days is fine.

2 Preheat the oven to 200°C (400°F/gas mark 6).

3 Remove the duck from the marinade, reserving the remaining liquid in a small pan. Dry the duck breasts well with kitchen paper, then season them all over with salt and the five-spice powder. Allow them to come back up to room temperature.

4 Heat a large heavy-based ovenproof frying pan (you may need two, depending on their size) until it's quite hot. Add the duck breasts, skin side down, reduce the heat to medium and cook for 3–4 minutes, until the skin is crisp and golden brown. Spoon off any excess fat.

5 Turn the duck breasts over and add the figs, tossing them to coat in the pan juices. Transfer the pan to the oven for 10 minutes, or a little longer if you don't like your duck too pink.

6 Meanwhile, bring the rest of the marinade to a simmer and reduce until slightly thickened.

7 Remove the duck and figs from the oven. Cover loosely with foil and leave to rest for 10 minutes.

8 Slice each duck breast on the diagonal and transfer each one to a warmed plate with the figs, then spoon over the reduced marinade. Put a bowl of steamed fragrant rice sprinkled with toasted sesame seeds alongside each one to serve.

Porchetta with Sautéed Potatoes

This classic Italian roast pork is traditionally served on special occasions like Christmas. I find that the shoulder has just the right balance of meat and fat.

SERVES 10–12

1 x 4kg (9lb) boneless shoulder of pork with rind

10 long fresh rosemary sprigs

75g (3oz) freshly grated Parmesan cheese

6 garlic cloves, finely chopped

6 tbsp chopped fresh flat-leaf parsley

For the sautéed potatoes:

1.4kg (3lb) small new potatoes, well scrubbed

175ml (6fl oz) olive oil

8 garlic cloves, lightly smashed and peeled

sea salt and freshly ground black pepper

1. Put the pork on a clean surface, cut loose any butcher's string and open it out. Roughly chop the leaves from three rosemary sprigs and sprinkle over the pork, then scatter over the Parmesan, garlic and parsley and season generously. Roll the pork back up tightly to enclose the filling completely.

2. Tie with butcher's string at 2cm (¾in) intervals to keep the meat in shape. If the skin is not already scored, use a small sharp knife to score the skin between the strings. Sprinkle with salt, then slip the remaining rosemary sprigs under the strings.

3. If you prefer it to have a softer, chewy skin, which is traditional, preheat the oven to 190°C (375°F/gas mark 5) and roast it straight away for 20 minutes per 500g (18oz) plus 20 minutes. For example, if your joint is exactly 4kg (9lb), it will take 3 hours. If you want it to have a crunchy crackling (this makes it harder to carve), leave it at room temperature for at least 2 hours and dry the excess water with kitchen paper before roasting. Cook as above, but increase the oven temperature to 220°C (425°F/gas mark 7) for the last 20 minutes of the cooking time. Remove from the oven and leave to rest for a good 30 minutes, as porchetta is best served warm rather than piping hot.

4. To sauté the potatoes, first cook them in a pan of boiling salted water for 15–20 minutes, until tender, then drain. When cool enough to handle, thinly slice. Heat the oil in a large frying pan (or two, depending on size) set over a fairly high heat. Add the garlic, followed by the potatoes. Allow to brown all over, tossing occasionally. Season to taste.

5. To serve, carve the porchetta into thin slices (an electric carving knife is very useful here) and arrange on warmed plates with the sautéed potatoes.

***

FABULOUS NO-MEAT DISHES

***

Salmon Coulibiac

This is a French adaptation of an old Russian recipe that can be made up to two days ahead. It's great for a buffet as it slices well and can be eaten with a fork.

SERVES 6–8

100g (4oz) butter, plus extra for greasing

550g (1¼lb) salmon fillet, boned and skinned

75g (3oz) basmati rice, well rinsed

225ml (8fl oz) fish or chicken stock

3 shallots, finely chopped

100g (4oz) small button mushrooms, thinly sliced

rind and juice of ½ lemon

2 large eggs

1 tbsp chopped fresh dill

2 tbsp chopped fresh flat-leaf parsley

500g (18oz) all-butter puff pastry, thawed if frozen

a little plain flour, for dusting

1 egg yolk mixed with 1 tbsp cream, to glaze

sea salt and freshly ground black pepper

green salad, to serve

cucumber pickle (page 178), to serve

1 Preheat the oven to 180°C (350°F/gas mark 4).

2 Butter a large piece of foil, put the salmon on it and season generously. Wrap up loosely into a parcel and put on a baking sheet. Roast in the oven for 15–20 minutes, then remove from the oven, open up the foil and allow it to cool completely.

3 Melt 25g (1oz) of the butter in a pan with a lid and stir in the rice. Cook for 1 minute, stirring, then pour in the stock and season. Bring to a simmer, then cover and cook for 10 minutes. Remove from the heat and leave to cool.

4 Meanwhile, melt 25g (1oz) of butter in a frying pan set over a low heat. Add the shallots and sauté for 10 minutes, until softened but not coloured. Add the mushrooms, season to taste and cook for another 5 minutes. Remove from the heat and stir in the lemon rind and juice. Leave to cool.

5 Put the eggs in a pan and cover with boiling water, then cook for 8 minutes to hard-boil. Drain and rinse under cold running water, then peel and chop.

6 Flake the salmon into a bowl. Add the hard-boiled eggs with the dill and half the parsley. Season to taste. In a separate bowl, mix the rice with the shallot and mushroom mixture and the rest of the parsley. Season to taste.

7 Roll out the pastry on a floured board to a 33cm (13in) square, then cut it into two lengths, one 15cm (6in) and the other 17.5cm (7in). Melt the remaining 50g (2oz) of butter and use to brush a large baking sheet. Put the smaller piece of pastry on the baking sheet and brush with melted butter too.

8 Spoon half of the rice mix down the centre of the pastry, leaving a 2.5cm (1in) border. Spoon the salmon mixture on top, building it into a firm loaf shape with your hands. Mould the remaining rice mix on top and brush the border with the egg glaze. Cover with the other piece of pastry and press around the edges to seal. Brush with the rest of the butter.

9 When you are ready to cook, preheat the oven to 220°C (425°F/gas mark 7) and brush the coulibiac with egg glaze. Bake in the oven for 25–30 minutes, until golden brown. Leave to rest for 10 minutes before cutting into slices to serve on plates with some salad and cucumber pickle.

Salmon Coulibiac, p.147

Cucumber Pickle, p.178

Filo-crusted Fish, Cheese & Leek Pie

This pie is perfect for putting straight on the table with a serving spoon and a large bowl of salad so that everyone can help themselves. It can be made up to 24 hours in advance and kept covered in the fridge until ready to bake.

SERVES 4–6

675g (1½lb) firm fish fillets (if using smoked fish, then preferably not dyed)

600ml (1 pint) milk

1 bay leaf

1 tsp black peppercorns

50g (2oz) butter, plus an extra knob

3 large leeks, trimmed and thinly sliced

50g (2oz) plain flour

2 tsp prepared English mustard

juice of ½ lemon

175g (6oz) mature Cheddar cheese, diced

watercress sprigs, to garnish

lemon wedges, to serve

For the filo topping:

100g (4oz) butter

2 large garlic cloves, crushed

4 sheets of filo pastry, thawed if frozen

2 tbsp very finely snipped fresh chives

sea salt and freshly ground black pepper

1 Put the fish in a sauté pan with the milk, bay leaf and peppercorns. Bring to a simmer, then turn off the heat, cover tightly with foil and set aside for 15 minutes, until the fish is cooked. Remove from the milk and break into bite-sized flakes, discarding the skin and any bones. Strain the milk into a jug and reserve.

2 Preheat the oven to 180°C (350°F/gas mark 4).

3 Heat a knob of butter in a pan set over a medium heat. Add the leeks and season to taste, then sauté for a couple of minutes, until just tender. Transfer to a 1.6 litre (2¾ pints) pie dish or similar that is about 22cm (8½in) in diameter.

4 Add the rest of the butter to the same pan. Once it has melted, stir in the flour and cook for 1 minute. Gradually add the reserved milk, stirring until you have a smooth sauce. Stir in the mustard and lemon to taste, then season.

5 To assemble, spoon one-third of the sauce over the leeks and scatter the fish on top, followed by another third of the sauce. Sprinkle over the cheese and cover with the rest of the sauce.

6 To make the topping, melt the butter in a small pan set over a low heat. Add the garlic and gently sauté for a few minutes. Lay one sheet of filo on a chopping board and brush with the garlic butter, then sprinkle over some chives and add a grinding of pepper. Put another sheet of filo on top at a slight angle and repeat. Continue until you have used up all the pastry, then put it on top of the pie, using a sharp knife to trim the edges but leave an overhang.

7 Bake in the oven for 35–40 minutes, until the pastry is crisp and golden brown. Garnish with watercress sprigs and serve straight to the table with the lemon wedges.

Valencian Seafood Paella

Traditionally, paella is made on a Sunday by the men in the family because women need a day off from cooking – sounds reasonable to me!

SERVES 4

3 tbsp extra virgin olive oil

8 large Dublin Bay prawns, shell on

1 onion, finely chopped

3 garlic cloves, finely chopped

2 vine-ripened tomatoes, grated and skin discarded

1 tsp sweet paprika

½ tsp hot smoked paprika (pimentón picante)

150g (5oz) baby squid, cleaned and cut into rings

200g (7oz) Spanish short grain rice, such as Calasparra, Bomba or paella rice

500ml (18fl oz) fish stock (from a jar, such as Ferrer)

good pinch of saffron strands, soaked in a little water

20 large live clams, cleaned

450g (1lb) raw peeled Dublin Bay or tiger prawns, cleaned

sea salt and freshly ground black pepper

lemon wedges, to garnish

1 Heat 1 tablespoon of the olive oil in a paella dish that is approximately 32cm (12½in) in diameter over a medium heat. Add the whole prawns and sauté for 2–3 minutes. Remove the prawns from the pan and set aside on a plate.

2 Heat the remaining 2 tablespoons of olive oil in the paella dish. Tip in the onion and garlic and sauté for a few minutes, until softened. Add the grated tomatoes and cook for 3–4 minutes, until reduced and thickened. Tip in the sweet and hot smoked paprika and cook for another minute, stirring. Add the squid and continue to sauté for a minute or so, then stir in the rice and stir to ensure it's all evenly coated.

3 Heat the stock in a separate pan. Pour 400ml (14fl oz) of it into the rice with the saffron mixture and season to taste. Increase the heat and simmer vigorously for 10 minutes, then arrange the sautéed whole prawns on top of the dish with the clams and raw peeled prawns, pushing them down into the rice but otherwise not disturbing it. Cook for about 8 minutes – if the dish looks very dry before the rice has cooked completely, then add the remaining hot stock, bearing in mind it shouldn't be soupy.

4 Cover the dish with foil and take off the heat. Leave to rest for 10 minutes, then garnish with lemon wedges and serve straight to the table.

Wild Mushroom Strudel

This is a wonderful combination of sautéed mushrooms and a crisp pastry crust. The filo pastry helps to keep the mushroom mixture really moist and full of flavour. The strudel can be prepared several hours in advance as long as it's tightly covered with cling film in the fridge and popped in the oven once your guests arrive – any longer and the filo will start to go soggy.

SERVES 4–6

2 tbsp rapeseed oil, plus extra for greasing

225g (8oz) mixed wild mushrooms, roughly chopped

1 small onion, finely chopped

2 garlic cloves, crushed

2 tbsp cream

2 tbsp Madeira

1 bunch of spring onions, trimmed and finely chopped

2 tbsp chopped fresh mixed herbs, such as basil, parsley and chives

4–5 sheets filo pastry, thawed if frozen (about 100g (4oz) in total)

1 egg, beaten

sea salt and freshly ground black pepper

mixed salad leaves with toasted hazelnuts, to serve

1. Preheat the oven to 190°C (375°F/gas mark 5). Line a baking sheet with non-stick baking paper.

2. Heat the oil in a large frying pan set over a high heat. Add the mushrooms, onion and garlic and cook for 2–3 minutes, until almost tender. Reduce the heat, pour in the cream and Madeira and cook for another minute. Add the spring onions, herbs and seasoning to taste. Sauté for another minute, until the spring onions are just tender and the liquid has almost completely reduced. Leave to cool.

3. Unroll the sheets of filo pastry and put them one on top of the other on a clean work surface. Brush the surface of the top sheet of pastry with beaten egg, then spread over the mushroom mixture to within 4cm (1½in) of the edge. Fold the short ends inwards, then starting with one long edge, roll up the pastry fairly tightly like you would a Swiss roll, keeping the mushrooms in place as you go. Put the strudel on the lined baking sheet, seam side down, and brush once more with the rest of the beaten egg. Bake in the oven for 20–25 minutes, until crisp and golden brown.

4. Leave to cool for a few minutes before sliding the strudel off the baking sheet onto a chopping board. Cut the strudel across and on the diagonal into 10 or 12 slices that are 4cm (1½in) thick. Arrange on warmed plates with some salad with toasted hazelnuts to serve.

Roast Butternut Squash, Kale & Goats' Cheese Salad with Puy Lentils

You could also make this salad with some shredded cooked turkey or ham and serve it on a large platter for everyone to share with some nice chewy multigrain sourdough bread – heaven!

SERVES 4–6

1 small butternut squash or pumpkin (about 1kg (2¼lb))

5 tbsp extra virgin olive oil

¼ tsp ground cumin

225g (8oz) dried Puy lentils

200g (7oz) kale, tough stalks removed and leaves shredded

2 shallots, finely chopped

1 garlic clove, crushed

1 tbsp red wine vinegar

large pinch of caster sugar

175g (6oz) goats' cheese log, cut into small cubes

25g (1oz) fresh flat-leaf parsley leaves, roughly chopped

4 tbsp snipped fresh chives

sea salt and freshly ground black pepper

fresh chive flowers, to garnish (optional)

multigrain sourdough bread, to serve

1 Preheat the oven to 200°C (400°F/gas mark 6).
2 Peel the butternut squash or pumpkin and remove the seeds, then cut the flesh into bite-sized pieces and place on a baking tray. Toss in 1 tablespoon of the olive oil and the cumin, then season to taste. Roast in the oven for 40–50 minutes, until softened and caramelised, tossing once or twice to ensure the pumpkin or squash cooks evenly.
3 Rinse the lentils in a sieve under cold running water, then put in a pan with 600ml (1 pint) of water. Add a pinch of salt and bring to the boil, then reduce the heat and simmer for 15–20 minutes, until al dente (tender but still with a little bite), adding the kale for the last 5 minutes of the cooking time. Drain and rinse well under cold running water.
4 Meanwhile, heat 1 tablespoon of the olive oil in a pan set over a medium heat and sauté the shallots for 4–5 minutes, until softened but not coloured. Tip into a bowl and stir in the cooked lentils with the remaining 3 tablespoons of olive oil and the garlic, red wine vinegar and sugar.
5 When the lentils have cooled to room temperature, gently fold in the goats' cheese with the parsley and chives, then season to taste. Finally, fold in the roasted pumpkin or butternut squash and heap onto a platter to serve. Garnish with chive flowers (if using). Have a separate basket of multigrain sourdough bread to hand around separately.

Barley Risotto with Creamed Carrots & Butternut

In Italy, an orzotto is a risotto that is cooked with barley instead of rice. Unlike risotto, it can happily be made up to three days in advance and indeed seems to only improve with time, making it a great vegetarian option.

SERVES 8–10

4 carrots, diced

1 small butternut squash, peeled, deseeded and diced

200ml (7fl oz) milk

50g (2oz) butter, plus an extra knob

1 tbsp rapeseed oil

1 onion, finely chopped

1 celery stick, finely chopped

500g (18oz) pearl barley

120ml (4fl oz) dry white wine

1.2 litres (2 pints) vegetable stock

100g (4oz) freshly grated Parmesan cheese

100g (4oz) cooked chestnuts, roughly chopped (optional)

25g (1oz) toasted raw pistachio nuts, roughly chopped

1 tbsp very finely snipped chives

sea salt and freshly ground black pepper

1 Preheat the oven to 200°C (400°F/gas mark 6).

2 Put the carrots in a pan with half of the butternut squash, the milk, a knob of butter and some seasoning. Put on a low heat, then cover with a lid and simmer for 30 minutes, until the carrots and squash are tender. Using a hand-held blender, blitz to a purée.

3 Put the rest of the butternut squash on a baking tray, toss with the rapeseed oil and season. Roast in the oven for 25–30 minutes, until tender, tossing occasionally to ensure the squash cooks evenly.

4 Melt the remaining butter in a sauté pan set over a low to medium heat. Add the onion and celery and sauté for about 10 minutes, until well softened but not coloured.

5 Increase the heat to high, add the barley and cook for 2–3 minutes, stirring, until it's giving off a nutty aroma. Add the wine and let it bubble down, still stirring.

6 Reduce the heat to low, then pour in the stock, cover with a lid and cook for 30–40 minutes, until the barley is tender, stirring once or twice to ensure it doesn't stick to the bottom of the pan. Fold in the carrot and squash purée and season to taste, then fold in the roasted squash with the Parmesan and chestnuts (if using), allowing them to warm through.

7 To serve, spoon into a warmed dish and scatter over the pistachios and chives.

Pecan Tart

This pecan tart has a bit of a kick, but you can of course leave the whiskey out if you're serving it to people who don't drink alcohol and/or kiddies.

SERVES 6–8

For the pastry:

250g (9oz) plain flour, plus extra for dusting

125g (4½oz) butter, chilled and cut into cubes

2 medium egg yolks

good pinch of salt

1–2 tbsp ice-cold water

For the filling:

175g (6oz) pecan nuts

3 medium eggs

150g (5oz) golden syrup

100g (4oz) butter

100g (4oz) dark soft brown sugar

50g (2oz) maple syrup

¼ tsp sea salt flakes

2 tbsp whiskey

seeds of ½ vanilla pod or 1 tsp vanilla extract

To serve:

vanilla ice cream

1 First make the pastry. Put the flour and butter in a food processor and blitz until it looks like fine breadcrumbs. Add the egg yolks and salt and blitz again until it forms a ball. If the mixture still looks a bit dry you can add the water, but you want a soft pastry that isn't sticky. Tip out onto a lightly floured surface and shape into a ball. Wrap in cling film and chill for 15 minutes to rest.

2 Preheat the oven to 180°C (350°F/gas mark 4).

3 Roll out the pastry on a lightly floured surface and use it to line a 10cm x 34cm (4in x 13½in) loose-bottomed flan tin that is 2.5cm (1in) deep. Put back in the fridge for 15 minutes to rest.

4 Meanwhile, put the pecans on a baking sheet and bake in the oven for 8–10 minutes, until lightly toasted. Remove from the oven and set aside 100g (4oz) of perfect whole ones, then roughly chop the rest to use in the filling.

5 Fill the lined pastry case with parchment paper and baking beans or dried kidney beans and put on a baking sheet. Bake in the oven for 15 minutes, until the pastry looks set but not coloured. Remove the beans and parchment. Separate one of the eggs (put the yolk to one side) and quickly brush the base with the unbeaten egg white to form a seal. Put back in to the oven for another 5 minutes, until the base is firm and the pastry feels sandy to the touch.

6 To make the filling, put the golden syrup, butter, sugar, maple syrup and salt in a pan set over a medium-high heat. Bring it to the boil, then turn down the heat and let it simmer for 3–5 minutes over a very low heat. Take off the heat and stir in the whiskey and vanilla and leave it to cool a little.

7 Add the eggs and reserved egg yolk one at a time, whisking well between each addition, then fold in the chopped pecans. Pour into the pastry case, then arrange the whole pecan nuts on top in attractive rows. Put the tart on a baking sheet, then bake in the oven for 15–20 minutes, until the filling is set but still has a little wobble. Leave to cool slightly, then cut into slices and serve warm on plate with a scoop of vanilla ice cream.

Mulled Winter Berry Victoria Sponge

This Victoria sponge is inspired by mulled wine and the fragrant scents that we all associate with Christmas. The jam is also delicious for breakfast, so consider making a double batch so that you can have some tucked away.

SERVES 6–8

For the sponge:

225g (8oz) butter, softened, plus extra for greasing

200g (7oz) caster sugar

4 medium eggs

225g (8oz) self-raising flour, sifted

finely grated rind of 2 oranges

seeds of ½ vanilla pod or 1 tsp vanilla extract

½ tsp ground cinnamon

¼ tsp baking powder

For the mulled berry jam:

300g (11oz) fresh or frozen mixed berries, such as blackberries, blackcurrants, blueberries and raspberries

250g (9oz) caster sugar

finely grated rind and juice of 1 orange

4 tbsp red wine

5 cardamom pods, bashed

2 star anise

1 cinnamon stick, snapped in half

¼ tsp ground ginger

To decorate:

450ml (¾ pint) cream

fresh mint leaves

1 Preheat the oven to 180°C (350°F/gas mark 4). Grease and line 2 x 20cm (8in) loose-bottomed cake tins with non-stick baking paper.

2 Using a hand-held electric mixer, cream together the butter and sugar in a large bowl. Add two of the eggs and half of the flour and beat until combined. Add the other two eggs and the rest of the flour along with the orange rind, vanilla, cinnamon and baking powder and beat vigorously to get a good amount of air into it.

3 Divide the batter between the prepared tins. Bake in the oven for 25–30 minutes, until the cakes have shrunk slightly from the sides of the tins and spring back when touched in the centre. Remove from the oven and leave the cakes to cool in the tins.

4 Meanwhile, make the mulled berry jam. Put all the ingredients in a heavy-based pan and heat gently until the sugar has dissolved. Put a small plate in the freezer (this is to check the jam later).

5 Raise the heat to medium and bring to the boil. Simmer for about 10 minutes, stirring regularly, until the liquid has reduced and the berries are coated in thick syrup. To check that the jam has reached setting consistency, remove the plate from the freezer and put a spoonful of jam on it. After a minute, push your finger through it. If it wrinkles, it's set. If not, give it another 5 minutes and check again. Leave to cool in the pan, then remove all the spices and discard.

6 Whisk the cream in a bowl until thickened and holding its shape. Put one sponge upside down on a serving plate or cake stand. Using a palette knife, spread on half of the whipped cream. Spoon over three-quarters of the jam, allowing some to drip over the edges, then cover with the second sponge. Pipe or swirl the rest of the whipped cream on top and dot with the remaining jam. Decorate with the fresh mint.

Almond & Lemon Curd Cake with Raspberry Sauce

With four layers, this cake is a real showstopper. The ground almonds help to keep it nice and moist, so it has good keeping properties.

SERVES 10–12

350g (12oz) butter, softened, plus extra for greasing

350g (12oz) caster sugar

6 large eggs

250g (9oz) self-raising flour

150g (5oz) ground almonds

finely grated rind of 3 lemons

For the filling and topping:

250g (9oz) fresh raspberries

juice of ½ lemon

1 tsp runny honey

300g (10oz) butter, softened

500g (18oz) icing sugar

1 vanilla pod, split in half lengthways and seeds scraped out

splash of milk

1–2 tbsp limoncello (shop-bought or see page 182)

300g (11oz) good-quality shop-bought lemon curd

1 Preheat the oven to 180°C (350°F/gas mark 4). Grease 2 x 20cm (8in) loose-bottomed cake tins and line with non-stick baking paper.

2 Using a hand-held electric mixer, cream together the butter and sugar in a large bowl. Beat in the eggs one at a time, then fold in the flour, ground almonds and lemon rind.

3 Divide the batter between the prepared tins. Bake in the oven for 35–40 minutes, until well risen and golden and a skewer inserted into the centre comes out clean. Leave to cool in the tins.

4 Meanwhile, reserve 100g (4oz) of the raspberries and mix the rest in a bowl with the lemon juice and honey. Leave at room temperature for 30 minutes, mashing occasionally, then push through a sieve to make a sauce.

5 To make the buttercream, using a hand-held electric mixer, beat the butter in a bowl until pale. Sift in half the icing sugar and beat for 1 minute, then sift in the rest. Add the vanilla and milk and beat for 3 minutes, until pale and creamy.

6 To assemble the cake, start by cutting each sponge in half so that you end up with four rounds. Put one on a plate or cake stand and add a few drops of limoncello before spreading over a thin layer of the buttercream, followed by a thin layer of lemon curd. Repeat until you've got four sponges stacked on top of each other. Spread the rest of the buttercream all over the top and sides of the cake, smoothing it nicely with a palette knife. Decorate with the reserved raspberries and serve the raspberry sauce in a little jug on the side. Cut into slices and arrange on plates to serve.

Red Velvet Tree Trunk Cake

This red velvet cake is so rich and moist, everyone will ask you for the recipe. It's the kind of cake where one slice could never possibly be enough, but it will keep well for a couple of days.

SERVES 12–20

For the sponge:

350g (12oz) soft light brown sugar

200g (7oz) butter, softened, plus extra for greasing

seeds of ½ vanilla pod or ½ tsp vanilla extract

½ tsp red food colouring

6 medium eggs

275g (10oz) self-raising flour

4 tbsp cocoa powder

1 tsp baking powder

200g (7oz) crème fraîche

For the frosting:

375g (13oz) icing sugar, sifted

175g (6oz) butter, softened

125g (4½oz) plain chocolate, melted

2 tbsp cream

For the chocolate ganache drizzle:

150ml (¼ pint) cream

150g (5oz) plain chocolate, chopped, plus extra for grating over the cake

1 Preheat the oven to 180°C (350°F/gas mark 4). Grease and line 3 x 20cm (8in) cake tins with non-stick baking paper.

2 In a freestanding mixer, cream the sugar and butter until light and fluffy, then beat in the vanilla and food colouring with two of the eggs. Add another two eggs and beat again, then beat in the last two eggs.

3 Sift together the flour, cocoa powder and baking powder. Using a large metal spoon, fold the dry ingredients into the creamed mixture in alternate batches with the crème fraîche.

4 Divide the batter between the prepared tins. Bake in the oven for 25–30 minutes, until well risen and a skewer inserted into the middle of each cake comes out clean. Leave to cool in the tins.

5 Mix together all the frosting ingredients in a freestanding mixer with a paddle attachment for 5 minutes, until light and spreadable. Put one of the cakes on a plate or cake stand with a blob of frosting underneath, then spread the top with a little more frosting. Cover with another cake and more frosting. Top with the remaining cake, but first flipping it over so that the flat side of the cake is now on top. Lightly press all the cake layers together, then use a palette knife to spread the remaining frosting over the top and sides of the cake, swirling it so it looks rough, like tree bark.

6 To make the chocolate ganache drizzle, heat the cream in a pan but don't boil it. Take off the heat and add the chocolate, leaving it to melt for a few minutes, then stir the chocolate gently and let it cool down a little. Pour the chocolate ganache drizzle all over the cake so that it drizzles in a nice smooth layer all over the top and then comes nicely down the sides of the cake. Grate over a little extra chocolate, cut into slices and arrange on plates to serve.

***

FESTIVE EXTRAS

***

Christmas Chocolate Mendiants

Mendiants are a traditional French confectionery that are made as part of the 13 Christmas desserts in the region of Provence. The custom is to top them with raisins, hazelnuts, dried figs and almonds to represent the four main monastic orders of the Dominicans, Augustinians, Franciscans and Carmelites. They make a fantastic last-minute gift or after-dinner sweet. You can of course replace the plain chocolate for white or milk if you prefer or make a selection of each one.

MAKES ABOUT 40

50g (2oz) whole cashew nuts

400g (14oz) plain chocolate (at least 70% cocoa solids), broken into squares

40g (1½oz) dried cranberries

40g (1½oz) crystallised ginger

1 Preheat the oven to 180°C (350°F/gas mark 4). Line two large baking sheets with non-stick baking paper.

2 Spread the cashew nuts on a baking sheet and roast in the oven for 6–8 minutes, until nicely toasted, stirring them halfway through to ensure they cook evenly. Remove from the oven and leave to cool completely.

3 Melt 325g (11½oz) of the chocolate in a heatproof bowl set over a pan of simmering water, making sure the water doesn't touch the bottom of the bowl. Stir occasionally until just melted, then take the pan off the heat and add the rest of the chocolate. Allow it to melt in the residual heat, stirring occasionally. Remove from the heat and leave to cool a little.

4 Using a teaspoon, pour little discs of the melted chocolate onto the lined baking sheets and use the back of the spoon to spread them out to a diameter of 2.5cm (1in). Do about four at a time because the toppings must be added while the chocolate is still soft. Gently press one cashew nut, two or three dried cranberries and one piece of crystallised ginger on the top of each chocolate disc.

5 Continue making the mendiants in the same way until all the chocolate has been used up. If the chocolate in the bowl begins to set a little before you have finished, simply put it back on the pan of simmering water and stir gently until just melted again. Allow the mendiants to set in a cool, dry place for 2–3 hours. Pop the chocolates into gift boxes or bags layered with tissue paper, tie with ribbon and share them. These can be made up to two weeks in advance if stored in an airtight container in a cool, dry place.

Preserved Lemons

You have probably seen recipes using preserved lemons, as Middle Eastern recipes are becoming more popular. This is a version of them that is extremely easy to make, and it looks so lovely once they've been packed into jars that you'll find yourself making extra to give as presents. My version has some sugar in the brine, but this gives the finished result a lovely sweet underdone.

MAKES 2 X 600ML (1 PINT) KILNER JARS

8 lemons

125g (4½oz) caster sugar

100g (4oz) sea salt flakes

1 tsp black peppercorns

1 tsp coriander seeds, lightly crushed

½ tsp cumin seeds, lightly crushed

¼ tsp ground turmeric

2 long fresh red chillies

2 bay leaves

2 fresh rosemary sprigs

1 Scrub the lemons clean and put in a pan covered with 750ml (1¼ pints) of water. Bring to the boil, then reduce the heat and simmer for 10–12 minutes, until softened. Using a slotted spoon, transfer the lemons to a bowl of iced water to cool them down quickly and prevent them from cooking any further.

2 Add the sugar and salt to the cooking liquid. Remove from the heat and stir in the peppercorns, coriander seeds, cumin seeds and turmeric. Pack the lemons into 2 x 600ml (1 pint) warm, sterilised Kilner jars and pour over enough of the brine to cover completely, then push a chilli, bay leaf and rosemary sprig down the side of each one before sealing tight. Store in a cool place or in the fridge for up to two weeks before using. To use, drain the lemons and finely dice the flesh.

Cucumber Pickle

I like to serve this with all types of smoked fish or just a chunk of mature Cheddar cheese. It benefits from being left for up to a month before using but is still delicious if you need to use it straight away. If you happen to grow your own vegetables, this is a fantastic way to use up a glut of cucumbers. I have also put fennel heads in from the garden when my fennel has gone to seed, as they not only look fantastic but have a lovely flavour as well.

MAKES 4 X 450ML (¾ PINT) KILNER JARS

3 cucumbers

3 large onions

salt, for sprinkling

450g (1lb) granulated sugar

1.5 litres (2½ pints) white wine vinegar

8 fresh bay leaves

15g (½oz) fresh fennel or dill, stems stripped into small sprigs

1 tbsp mixed peppercorns

1 tbsp coriander seeds, toasted

2 tsp black mustard seeds

2 tsp black onion seeds

1 tsp dried chilli flakes

1 Slice the cucumbers and onions on a mandolin and layer up in a colander, sprinkling with salt as you go. Set aside for a couple of hours, then rinse well under cold running water. Leave to drain, then pat dry with kitchen paper.

2 Put the sugar and vinegar in a pan and bring to the boil, then boil fast for 3 minutes. Remove from the heat.

3 Pack the cucumbers and onions into 4 x 450ml (¾ pint) warm, sterilised Kilner jars, layering them up with the herbs and spices to within 1cm (½in) from the top of the jars. Ladle in enough of the vinegar and sugar liquid to cover completely. Seal and store in a cool, dark place for up to three months or until needed. Once opened, keep in the fridge and use as required.

Grape Chutney

If you're looking for something a bit different that you can't buy in the shops, then this preserve is perfect. It goes brilliantly with my chicken liver parfait (page 32) but is also great served with cold cuts over the festive period, particularly turkey or a nice mature cheese. It would be the most fantastic present presented in a hamper that has been filled with straw with a fresh ham and a nice linen tea towel.

MAKES ABOUT 4 X 450ML (¾ PINT) KILNER JARS

5 Granny Smith apples, peeled, cored and diced

150ml (¼ pint) balsamic vinegar

150ml (¼ pint) brandy (preferably Cognac)

1 onion, finely chopped

1kg (2¼lb) white seedless grapes

175g (6oz) Demerara sugar

1 tsp mixed spice

1 tsp ground cinnamon

½ tsp ground ginger

good pinch of sea salt

Put the apples in a large heavy-based pan with the vinegar and brandy and cook for 30 minutes over a low heat. Stir in the onion, grapes, sugar, spices and salt and continue to simmer for 1½ hours, stirring occasionally, until the mixture is thick and pulpy. Leave to cool slightly, then spoon into 4 x 450ml (¾ pint) warm, sterilised Kilner jars and seal. Store in a cool, dark place for up to three months or until needed. Once open, keep in the fridge and use as required.

Redcurrant Vodka

Ideally this should be made in the summer when you've got a glut of redcurrants from the garden, but if you're not that organised, look for the frozen variety, as they will also work really well. Use this vodka as a basis for cocktails or just serve well chilled in shot glasses as a novel Christmas drink to get the party started! You could also use this method to make your own sloe gin or crème de cassis.

MAKES ABOUT 1 LITRE (1¾ PINTS)

750g (1lb 10oz) redcurrants
750ml (1¼ pints) vodka
300g (11oz) granulated sugar

1   Put the redcurrants and vodka in a large warm, sterilised Kilner jar. Seal tightly and put in a cool, dark place for at least one month, but up to three months is ideal. Once the redcurrants have been left for a time to steep in the vodka, you will notice that the vodka will start to take on their colour.
2   Carefully pour the whole lot into a large bowl. Using a potato masher, mash the fruit, extracting as much of the flavour and colour as possible. Pour into a large sieve lined with muslin or use a jelly sieve, or even a clean pillowcase suspended on a broom handle between two chairs. Allow the liquid to drip through overnight, but don't be tempted to give it a gentle push or it will make the vodka cloudy.
3   Put the sugar in a heavy-based pan with 150ml (¼ pint) of water. Set over a low heat and simmer gently until the sugar has dissolved. Remove from the heat and pour enough into the strained vodka to taste. Using a funnel, transfer into warm, sterilised bottles and either use straight away or store in a cool, dark place for up to three months. Use as required.

Limoncello

Most people have encountered this digestif if they've been lucky enough to go to Italy on their holidays. It's perfect in my almond and lemon curd cake (see page 171).

MAKES ABOUT 1 LITRE (1¾ PINTS)

finely grated rind and juice of 8 lemons (unwaxed and organic, if possible)
675g (1½lb) granulated sugar
750ml (1¼ pints) vodka

Put the lemon rind in a large pan with the sugar and 500ml (18fl oz) of water. Heat gently until the sugar dissolves, then increase the heat slightly and simmer for 15 minutes. Take the pan off the heat and stir in the lemon juice and vodka, then cover and leave to infuse for one week. Strain and store as described above. Use as required.

Spiced Cranberry Florentines

This is a lovely variation of regular Florentines. It uses star anise, which you can buy in Asian markets and most supermarkets nowadays. I recommend that you grind it fresh using either a spice grinder or a pestle and mortar.

MAKES 16

4 tbsp light brown sugar

4 tbsp softened butter

1 tbsp honey

½ tsp ground star anise

pinch of ground nutmeg

pinch of sea salt

75g (3oz) dried cranberries, finely chopped

50g (2oz) blanched almonds, finely chopped

4 tbsp plain flour

75g (3oz) plain chocolate (at least 70% cocoa solids), broken into squares

1 Preheat the oven to 180°C (350°F/gas mark 4). Line two large baking sheets with non-stick baking paper.

2 Put the sugar, butter, honey, star anise, nutmeg and salt in a pan. Set the pan over a low heat until the butter melts, stirring with a wooden spoon. Remove from the heat and mix in the cranberries, almonds and flour.

3 Put heaped teaspoons of the cranberry and almond mixture onto the prepared baking sheets, making sure you space them apart as they will spread quite a bit in the oven. Bake in the oven for 8–10 minutes, until the Florentines have spread a little and are golden brown. Leave to cool completely on the baking sheets.

4 Once the Florentines have cooled, melt the chocolate in a heatproof bowl set over a pan of simmering water or in the microwave. Using a palette knife, flip the Florentines over and drizzle the melted chocolate over them. Leave to set for a couple of minutes before serving or storing.

5 These will keep happily in alternating rows of chocolate side up in an airtight container for up to two weeks. If you would like to give them to someone as a gift, simply pack into a Kilner jar or gift box in layers of tissue paper.

Mint Chocolate Truffles

These truffles will make wonderful gifts for friends – if you can bear to give them away, that is! For a different flavour, add rum, Cointreau or whiskey instead of the crème de menthe and mint or experiment with different coatings, such as grated chocolate or finely chopped pistachio nuts or toasted almonds.

MAKES 30

120ml (4fl oz) cream

1 tbsp chopped fresh mint

1 tbsp crème de menthe

225g (8oz) plain chocolate (at least 70% cocoa solids), broken into squares

For the coating:

50g (2oz) plain chocolate (at least 70% cocoa solids), broken into squares

25g (1oz) good-quality cocoa powder

1 Put the cream in a small pan with the mint and crème de menthe. Bring to the boil, then remove from the heat and allow to cool. Set aside for 1 hour to allow the flavours to infuse.

2 Pour the infused cream through a fine sieve into a small clean pan and bring to the boil. Reduce the heat, then whisk in the chocolate until smooth and melted. Put in a bowl, cover with cling film and leave to cool in the fridge for 2–3 hours, until the mixture is cold and set.

3 Remove the bowl from the fridge about 30 minutes before you intend to finish the truffles. Scoop into 30 even-sized balls – a large melon baller works best for this. Make sure to dip the melon baller in hot water between each scoop to make the job easier. Arrange on a baking sheet lined with non-stick baking paper. Wearing clean rubber gloves and with cold hands, roll the balls into slightly more rounded shapes. Chill while preparing the final stage.

4 To make the coating, melt the chocolate in a heatproof bowl set over a pan of simmering water or in the microwave, then leave to cool a little. Sift the cocoa into a small bowl. Again, wearing clean rubber gloves, dip the tips of your fingers in the melted chocolate and rub it all over a truffle to lightly coat. Toss in the cocoa powder until completely coated, then arrange on a clean baking sheet lined with non-stick baking paper. Repeat until all the truffles are coated, cover with cling film and chill until needed.

5 Pop the chocolate truffles into gift boxes or bags with tissue paper, tie with ribbon and share them. These will keep happily in the fridge for up to two weeks. To serve, arrange the truffles on a plate or platter.

Antipasti Platter with Spiced Nuts & Marinated Olives

Whether you're planning on gathering your family together before going out to an event or having a small get together at home, everyone likes to have something to nibble on. This deliciously informal antipasti platter looks stunning when served like this.

SERVES 4–6

6 slices of Parma ham

225g (8oz) piece of Italian cheese, such as dolcelatte or taleggio, cut into slices

25g (1oz) wild rocket

1 tbsp extra virgin olive oil

½ tsp balsamic vinegar

bruschetta, slices of crusty bread or crackers, to serve

For the olives:

1 tsp cumin seeds

1 tsp fennel seeds

225g (8oz) black or green olives or a mixture (from a jar or can)

2 garlic cloves, crushed

finely grated rind and juice of 1 small lemon

4 tbsp extra virgin olive oil

1 tsp dried chilli flakes (optional)

For the nuts:

4 tbsp softened butter

225g (8oz) roasted salted whole almonds

4 tbsp soft light brown sugar

good pinch of sweet or smoked paprika

sea salt and freshly ground black pepper

1 To marinate the olives, toast the cumin and fennel seeds in a small dry frying pan for 1–2 minutes, until they become aromatic. Tip into a bowl and add the olives, garlic, lemon rind and juice, olive oil and chilli flakes (if using). Toss until each olive is well coated, then leave to marinate for at least 15 minutes (or for as long as time allows) to let the flavours develop.

2 To make the spiced nuts, melt the butter in a large frying pan set over a medium-high heat. Add the almonds and toss to coat, then sprinkle over the sugar and add the paprika with a good pinch of salt and pepper. Cook for about 5 minutes, stirring constantly, until the almonds are golden brown and the sugar has caramelised. Spread out on a baking sheet lined with non-stick baking paper to cool and harden.

3 To serve, drain off the excess liquid from the olives and tip into small bowls set on a larger platter. Break up the spiced almonds before piling into bowls and adding those to the platter along with the Parma ham and slices of cheese. Lightly dress the rocket with the oil and vinegar and pile that onto the platter to serve with the bruschetta, bread or crackers.

Amelda's Perfect Sausage Rolls

These sausage rolls are hard to beat and are Amelda's go-to recipe when we make them for a family gathering or a party, as everyone absolutely loves them. They are ideal to prepare in advance, as they can be frozen, uncooked and layered between sheets of parchment paper in a plastic container, for up to one month. If you want to cook them from frozen, simply increase the cooking time by about 10 minutes.

MAKES 16 SMALL SAUSAGE ROLLS

500g (18oz) good-quality sausagemeat

50g (2oz) sun-dried tomatoes in oil, drained and finely chopped

1 small onion, finely chopped

4 tbsp freshly grated Parmesan cheese

3 tbsp chopped fresh flat-leaf parsley

500g (18oz) all-butter puff pastry, thawed if frozen

plain flour, for dusting

1 egg

1 tbsp milk

2 tsp sesame seeds

sea salt and freshly ground black pepper

tomato ketchup, to serve

1. Preheat the oven to 200°C (400°F/gas mark 6). Line two baking sheets with non-stick baking paper.
2. To make the filling, put the sausagemeat in a bowl and mix with the sun-dried tomatoes, onion, Parmesan and parsley. Season to taste.
3. Roll out the pastry on a lightly floured work surface to make a long oblong shape that measures 35cm x 33cm (14in x 13in), then cut the pastry in half again lengthways. Form half of the sausagemeat filling into a long log shape that will run the whole length of the pastry, then put it on top of the pastry, making sure it's approximately 5mm (¼in) from the edge. Break the egg into a bowl and add the milk and a pinch of salt, then lightly beat together to make an egg wash. Brush the sides of the pastry with the egg wash, then fold the pastry over to enclose the filling and press down well to seal the edges, either crimping them with your fingers or pressing down with a fork. Repeat with the rest of the pastry and filling.
4. Cut each long sausage roll into eight bite-sized pieces, trimming down and discarding the ends. Glaze the sausage rolls with the rest of the egg wash, then sprinkle each one lightly with sesame seeds and arrange on the lined baking sheets.
5. Bake in the oven for 15–20 minutes, until cooked through and lightly golden, swapping the baking sheets around on the oven shelves halfway through. Arrange on plates or a large platter and serve hot or cold with tomato ketchup.

Cheat's Canapés

As we well know in the restaurant, canapés can take a lot of time and expertise to make. It can be difficult to estimate the correct amount you'll need, but these little numbers are a great shortcut. Mix up the type of tortilla chips you use according to the toppings, and if spooning small amounts onto each one seems like too much work, then simply use the toppings as dips. Make them up just before you need them – perfect for when the family drops in unannounced!

MAKES ABOUT 150

3 x 200g (7oz) packets of tortilla chips (choose from chilli, lightly salted, plain or blue)

fresh micro herbs, to garnish

For the chilli crab:

275g (10oz) fresh white crabmeat

2 spring onions, very finely chopped

1 small mild fresh red chilli, deseeded and finely chopped

4 tbsp sour cream

2 tbsp chopped fresh coriander

squeeze of lime juice

For the guacamole:

2 firm, ripe avocados

squeeze of lemon juice

1 heaped tbsp mayonnaise

6 ripe baby plum tomatoes, finely chopped

½ small garlic clove, crushed

few drops of Tabasco sauce

For the smoked salmon pâté:

150g (5oz) smoked salmon (trimmings are fine)

200g (7oz) soft cream cheese

1 heaped tbsp crème fraîche

squeeze of lemon juice

small bunch of fresh chives or dill, very finely chopped

sea salt and freshly ground black pepper

1 To make the chilli crab, put the crabmeat in a bowl and mix with the spring onions, chilli, sour cream, coriander and lime juice and season to taste. This can be made up to 2 hours in advance and kept covered in the fridge until needed.

2 To make the guacamole, cut the avocados in half and remove the stones, then scoop the flesh into a bowl. Mash with the lemon juice and mayonnaise. Stir in the tomatoes, garlic and Tabasco and season to taste. Cover with cling film and chill for up to 2 hours.

3 To make the smoked salmon pâté, chop the smoked salmon into small pieces. Tip the cream cheese and crème fraîche into a food processor and add the lemon juice. Season with pepper and blitz to your liking. Add the smoked salmon and pulse a few times if you want the pâté chunky or blitz some more if you want a pâté that's smooth and pink. Stir in the herbs and transfer to a bowl, then cover and chill until needed.

4 Just before serving, spoon teaspoonfuls of the toppings on each tortilla chip, garnish with micro herbs and arrange on platters.

Crispy Chicken Wings with Blue Cheese Dip

These American classics are ridiculously crispy on the outside and so juicy on the inside. They're great to serve for an informal night in front of the TV – the only problem is that there never seems to be enough to go around!

SERVES 4–6

vegetable oil, for deep-frying

1.4kg (3lb) chicken wings, at room temperature

75g (3oz) cornflour

1 tsp celery salt

1 tsp garlic powder

1 tsp cayenne pepper

4 celery sticks, trimmed and cut into thin sticks

For the dip:

100g (4oz) blue cheese, crumbled

4 tbsp mayonnaise

4 tbsp sour cream

4 tbsp buttermilk

1 tbsp lemon juice

1 tsp chopped fresh flat-leaf parsley

For the sauce:

120ml (4fl oz) hot pepper sauce, such as Frank's RedHot

1 tsp celery salt

1 tsp garlic powder

½ tsp cayenne pepper (optional)

50g (2oz) butter, melted

2 tbsp apple cider vinegar

1 To make the blue cheese dip, blend all the ingredients together except the parsley in a bowl with a hand-held blender, then stir in the parsley and season to taste. Cover with cling film and chill until needed. This can be made up to two days in advance.

2 Heat the oil in a deep-fat fryer to 190°C (375°F) and put the oven on a low heat.

3 Using a sharp knife, discard the wing tip and keep the little drum and wingette together. Put the cornflour in a bowl with the celery salt, garlic powder and cayenne pepper. Mix well, then use to coat the chicken, shaking off any excess. Deep-fry in batches for 10–12 minutes, until crisp and golden brown. Transfer to a wire rack set on a baking sheet and keep warm in the oven while you cook the rest.

4 To make the sauce, mix the hot sauce with the celery salt, garlic powder and cayenne (if using), then stir in the melted butter and vinegar. Pour the sauce into a small pan and allow to just warm through.

5 Once all the chicken wings are cooked, toss them in enough of the warmed sauce to coat, allowing any excess to drain off. Serve at once piled high in a bowl with the blue cheese dip and the celery sticks alongside. Have plenty of napkins for those sticky fingers!

Oat & Cranberry Cookies

These cookies are irresistible when warm and are perfect for serving on Christmas night. The dried cranberries can be replaced with raisins or chopped dried apricots, depending on what you fancy. Once you have added the flour, bring the cookie dough together using as few stirs as possible so that the dough doesn't get too tough.

MAKES 10

100g (4oz) butter, softened

100g (4oz) light brown sugar

1 egg

2 tsp vanilla extract

130g (4½oz) porridge oats

75g (3oz) dried cranberries

50g (2oz) self-raising flour

½ tsp ground cinnamon

1 Preheat the oven to 180°C (350°F/gas mark 4). Line two baking sheets with non-stick baking paper.

2 Cream the butter and sugar in a large bowl with a wooden spoon. Beat in the egg and vanilla, then stir in the oats, cranberries, flour and cinnamon.

3 Divide the cookie dough into 10 equal-sized blobs (each about 50g (2oz)), placing them on the prepared baking sheets as you go and leaving plenty of space for them to spread out.

4 Bake in the oven for 8–10 minutes. The trick is to pull them out of the oven before they are super firm – you want them to come out just slightly underbaked so that when they cool they will still be chewy. Remove from the oven and leave to cool a little before serving.

Snowman Cake

When we were in the planning stages of this book, my publisher, Nicki Howard, told us with great enthusiasm about a snowman cake that she made every year as part of their family tradition. She has very kindly shared the recipe with me and this is it!

SERVES 8–10

175g (6oz) butter, softened, plus extra for greasing

175g (6oz) caster sugar

3 eggs

225g (8oz) self-raising flour

2 tbsp milk

For the buttercream:

225g (8oz) icing sugar, sifted

75g (3oz) butter, softened

2 tbsp milk

To decorate:

75g (3oz) desiccated coconut

400g (14oz) marzipan

a few drops of red food colouring

a few drops of black food colouring

icing sugar, for dusting

a small handful of sultanas

1 glace cherry

1 Preheat the oven to 160°C (325°F/gas mark 3). Grease one 200ml (7fl oz) metal or Pyrex pudding basin and one 600ml (1 pint) metal or Pyrex pudding basin with butter.

2 Using a hand-held electric mixer, beat the butter and sugar together until soft and fluffy. Beat in the eggs one at a time, then fold in the flour. Stir in the milk to make a cake batter with a soft consistency.

3 Put one-quarter of the cake batter into the small greased pudding basin and put the rest into the large one. Put the cakes in the oven and bake the smaller one for 40 minutes, until golden brown and a skewer pushed right into the centre comes out clean. The larger cake will take about 1 hour and 10 minutes.

4 To make the buttercream, whisk all the ingredients together until you have a smooth icing. Cover with cling film and set aside at room temperature until needed.

5 Leave the cakes to cool in the basins, then turn out onto a clean board. Cut a thin slice from the side of each basin cake to make a flat base. Cut a similar slice from the opposite side of the larger cake. If you want to ensure that the cake is going to be really secure while you decorate it, use a 20cm (8in) wooden skewer to make a hole in the head and body, then position it so that it holds the body and head together securely. Put a small amount of the buttercream on a 25cm (10in) round cake board and use the rest to coat the snowman completely. Gently roughly it up with a knife, then dust with the coconut, gently brushing away any excess.

6 Colour one-quarter of the marzipan with the red food colouring and roll it out on a clean work surface lightly dusted with icing sugar. Using a small sharp knife, cut into a scarf that can be tied around the snowman's neck. Colour the rest of the marzipan with the black food colouring and shape it into a hat and two eyes. Use the glace cherry for a nose. This will keep well for up to two days if stored in a cool, dark place before serving.

Mini Croque Monsieurs

These can be made the day before you need them and covered with cling film until ready to bake. Feel free to substitute the Cheddar cheese with any other cheese you have to hand or you could even use a mixture. If the cheese is too soft to grate, then cut it into very fine dice.

MAKES ABOUT 30

150g (5oz) Cheddar cheese, such as Wexford mature, grated

200ml (7fl oz) crème fraîche

1 tsp mild mustard

10 thick slices of white or brown bread

about 225g (8oz) cooked wafer-thin ham (or use leftover Christmas ham – see pages 44 or 47)

about 3 tbsp softened butter

sea salt and freshly ground black pepper

1 Preheat the oven to 190°C (375°F/gas mark 5).

2 Mix together 100g (4oz) of the cheese with the crème fraîche and mustard. Season with salt and pepper and spread half of the mixture over five slices of the bread. Cover with a layer of the cooked ham and finish each one with another slice of the bread.

3 Thinly spread the butter over one side of each sandwich, then arrange on a baking sheet, buttered side down. Spread the rest of the butter over the tops of the sandwiches and sprinkle the remaining cheese on top.

4 Bake in the oven for 15–20 minutes, until golden, then cut into bite-sized pieces, removing the crusts if liked. Arrange on a platter, then pierce each one with a cocktail stick and serve immediately.

Chorizo with Celeriac Remoulade

The remoulade can be made a day in advance and kept covered in the fridge. For variety, substitute half the celeriac for red-skinned pears or apples and add some chopped fresh flat-leaf parsley if you've got any to hand.

MAKES 40

1 small celeriac

juice of 1 lemon

1 tbsp mild mustard

2–3 tbsp mayonnaise or crème fraîche

40 thin slices of chorizo, preferably Gubbeen Smokehouse, rind removed

sea salt and freshly ground black pepper

1 Peel the celeriac, then coarsely grate it in a food processor or shred into matchsticks on a mandolin. Put in a bowl with the lemon juice, mustard and enough of the mayonnaise or crème fraîche to bind. Season with salt and pepper.

2 To serve, spoon a teaspoon of the celeriac remoulade on each slice of chorizo, then fold over to encase the remoulade and secure with a cocktail stick.

Smoked Trout Rolls with Cream Cheese & Red Onion

These make great canapés for a party and are also a useful starter that can be made ahead of time. We are lucky enough to have a great smoked trout supplier in Ireland, Goatsbridge Trout Farm in Co. Kilkenny. It's run by Mag and Ger Kirwan, who have done a fantastic job of promoting their product to both chefs and consumers.

SERVES 4

1 small red onion, finely diced

75g (3oz) soft cream cheese

2 tbsp crème fraîche

1 tbsp snipped fresh chives

350g (12oz) sliced smoked trout

8 large slices of wheaten bread

sea salt and freshly ground black pepper

lemon slices, to garnish

1 Put the red onion in a small bowl and pour over enough boiling water to cover, then drain off immediately. This softens the raw flavour of the onion.

2 Return the red onion to the bowl and add the cream cheese, crème fraîche and chives. Season to taste and mix well to combine.

3 Put three overlapping slices of smoked trout on a sheet of cling film. Spread the cream cheese mixture a few millimetres thick over the top of the trout, right out to the edges. Roll up into a neat sausage shape. Repeat this process with the remaining slices of trout and cream cheese filling. Keep chilled in the fridge until ready to serve.

4 Using a straight-sided scone cutter that is about 5cm (2in) in diameter, cut out two rounds from each slice of wheaten bread (you could use the leftovers in brown bread ice cream).

5 Slice each chilled smoked trout roll into four small rounds and lay each roll sideways on a bread round. Arrange on a platter and garnish with the lemon slices to serve.

Baby Gem Cups with Prawns & Mango

This fresh, light canapé will complement any canapé selection. Just don't let them hang around for too as they will lose their crispness and begin to wilt.

MAKES 20

2 heads of Little Gem lettuce

300g (11oz) cooked and peeled Dublin Bay prawns

1 large firm, ripe mango, peeled and cut into small dice

juice of 1 lime

about 2 tbsp olive oil

sea salt and freshly ground black pepper

fresh micro herbs, to garnish

1 Divide the Little Gems into individual leaves, trimming down the large outside leaves so that they are all roughly the same size – you'll need 20 in total. Put in a large bowl and cover with cling film. Chill until ready to use. Use the very small centre leaves in a sandwich or for another dish.

2 Chop the Dublin Bay prawns if large and put in a bowl with the mango and lime juice. Dress with the olive oil, mixing well to combine, and season to taste. Cover with cling film and chill until ready to use – you can prepare this up to 4 hours in advance.

3 To serve, arrange the Little Gem leaves on a serving platter. Spoon in a little of the prawn and mango mixture and finish each one with a few micro herbs.

Blinis with Smoked Salmon

Blinis are originally from Russia and are perfect topped with sour cream, smoked salmon, dill and whatever caviar you can afford! Of course, if you don't have time to make your own, most supermarkets stock a range of ready-made cocktail-sized blinis, particularly during the festive season.

MAKES 30–40

225g (8oz) smoked salmon slices
200ml (7fl oz) sour cream
1–2 tbsp chopped fresh dill
fresh micro herbs, to garnish
salmon caviar, to serve (optional)

For the blinis:
175g (6oz) plain flour
50g (2oz) buckwheat flour
1 tsp fine sea salt
1 x 7g sachet of fast-action dried yeast
225ml (8fl oz) milk
200ml (7fl oz) crème fraîche
2 large eggs, separated
groundnut oil, for greasing
40g (1½oz) butter

1 First make the blinis. Sift the flours into a large bowl and add the salt and yeast. Heat the milk and crème fraîche to lukewarm in a medium pan. Whisk in the egg yolks, then add the flour mixture. Mix into a dough, then transfer to an oiled bowl and cover with cling film. Leave to rise for 1 hour in a warm place, until doubled in size.

2 When the dough has doubled in size, whisk the egg whites in a separate bowl, then fold them into the dough and leave to rise for another hour.

3 When you're ready to cook the blinis, heat a large non-stick frying pan or flat griddle pan over a medium heat and smear with a little of the butter. Ladle tablespoons of the blini mix into the pan, then add another heaped teaspoonful to each one to make the middle thicker. Turn when firm and cook until lightly brown. Leave to cool on a wire rack.

4 Pile up the slices of smoked salmon into a stack (or you could shape into rosettes if you prefer). Using a very sharp knife, cut across the stack to make thin strips. Smear a little of the sour cream on each blini and arrange the smoked salmon on top. Add a tiny dollop of the sour cream to each one and garnish with the dill and micro herbs and a little caviar (if using). Serve at once.

Sticky Cocktail Sausages with Sesame Seeds

These are completely irresistible and can be served hot or cold, so they're great party food and easy buffet fare. Hand around a separate dish for used cocktail sticks.

SERVES 4–6

20 cocktail sausages (about 350g (12oz) in total)

2 tbsp hoisin or plum sauce

2 tsp dark soy sauce

2 tsp runny honey

1 tsp wholegrain mustard

1 tbsp sesame seeds

1 Preheat the oven to 200°C (400°F/gas mark 6).

2 Put the sausages in a non-stick roasting tray in a single layer. Mix together the hoisin or plum sauce, soy sauce, honey, mustard and 2 teaspoons of water in a bowl, then pour over the sausages, turning to coat.

3 Bake the sausages in the oven for 15 minutes, then drain off any excess fat and sprinkle over the sesame seeds. Cook for another 5–10 minutes, until golden and sticky.

4 To serve, arrange on a warmed plate skewered with cocktail sticks.

***

CHRISTMAS DRINKS

***

Mocktails

Choose from this selection of refreshing, Christmassy mocktails that still have plenty of cheer for the designated driver or for those who are too young or might not want to drink alcohol but still want to raise a glass.

Seasonal Breeze
Mix together equal quantities of smooth orange and cranberry juice and slowly top up with a sparkling elderflower drink, as it will fizz up. Stir to combine and pour into tall glasses half-filled with ice to serve.

Blissful Blueberry
Half-fill tall glasses with blueberry juice and add a good squeeze of lemon or lime juice to each one. Top up with soda water, then add a handful of ice cubes and a couple of fresh blueberries to each one if you've got them.

Mistletoe
Half-fill tall glasses with ice, then add a dash of lime cordial to each one. Top up with ginger beer and add a squeeze of lime juice to each one. Decorate with a lime wedge.

Christmas Cranberry & Pineapple Punch
Mix together equal quantities of cranberry and pineapple juice and top up with ginger ale. Pour into tall glasses half-filled with ice and decorate with lime slices and fresh cranberries.

Mulled Wine

You may need to alter the amount of sugar you use depending on how sweet your orange juice is. Just be careful that you don't allow the mixture to boil or you'll cook off the alcohol and ruin the appearance of the lemon and orange slices. Christmas is one of those celebrations when children are the heart of the event, so you could replace the wine with sparkling red grape juice so that everyone can enjoy this yummy drink.

SERVES 4–6

1 bottle of red wine

600ml (1 pint) freshly squeezed orange juice

100g (4oz) caster sugar

1 lemon, halved and sliced

1 orange, halved and sliced

2 cinnamon sticks, broken in half

12 whole cloves

6 whole star anise

1 Put all the ingredients in a pan and heat gently for about 5 minutes, stirring occasionally, until the sugar has dissolved and the flavours have combined.

2 Ladle the mulled wine into heatproof glasses, making sure that some of the orange and lemon slices go into each one to serve.

Warm White Wine with Honey and Herbs

Not everyone is a fan of the complex flavours of traditional mulled wine, so this is something warming for white wine drinkers that will still take the chill out of the night. It would also work brilliantly with a nice artisan dry cider.

SERVES 6

1 bottle of dry white wine (I like to use a Sauvignon Blanc)

finely grated rind and juice of 1 lemon

1 small bunch of fresh thyme

1 small bunch of fresh rosemary

2 tbsp honey

Put all the ingredients in a heavy-based pan. Heat gently until just simmering, then pour into warmed glasses to serve.

Homemade Spice Sachets

This is my favourite combination of spices and flavourings for a delicious Irish whiskey punch, but it could also be used for mulled wine or cider. It has the perfect balance of spices so that no single ingredient is too overpowering. They are lovely little Christmas presents for friends and neighbours when decorated with ribbon and attached to a bottle of red wine.

MAKES 6 SACHETS ....

24 fresh thyme sprigs

18 cardamom pods

6 cinnamon sticks

6 pared pieces of orange rind (use a potato peeler)

6 tsp whole cloves

6 tsp juniper berries

Lay 6 x 15cm (6in) squares of muslin or cheesecloth out flat on a clean surface and divide the ingredients evenly between them. Gather up the edges, then tie each square into a neat bag with a piece of string.

Irish Whiskey Punch

This doesn't need to be made with your finest whiskey, as there are plenty of other complex flavours going on. I guarantee it will lift your spirits if you are feeling a little under the weather.

SERVES 1 ....

4 tbsp Irish whiskey

2 tsp light brown sugar

1 spice sachet (see recipe above)

fresh thyme sprig, to decorate

Put the whiskey and sugar into a tall sturdy glass. Add the spice sachet and fill with boiling water, stirring to dissolve the sugar and infuse the spice bag. Decorate with a thyme sprig and serve immediately, preferably in front of a roaring fire!

Raspberry & Lime Cordial

This is a lovely drink to have tucked away for Christmas. It's delicious topped up with soda water and ice or perhaps even some well-chilled Cava or Prosecco. I find it works best when you use one part cordial to four parts water or alcohol. The cordial will keep unopened for a few months. Once opened, store in the fridge for up to two weeks.

MAKES ABOUT 750ML (1¼ PINTS)

675g (1½lb) raspberries
500g (18oz) caster sugar
juice of 2 limes

1 Put the raspberries in a pan with the sugar and lime juice. Mash the berries, then set the pan over a low heat for 10 minutes, until smooth and syrupy. Rub through a sieve into a clean pan.

2 Tip the seeds from the sieve into a bowl and stir in 300ml (½ pint) of water, then sieve again to remove the last of the pulp from the seeds. Pour the liquid into the pan with the sieved pulp, stir well and boil for 1 minute. Pour into a warm sterilised bottle and seal. Use as required.

Hot Chocolate with Marshmallows

Hot chocolate should be wickedly rich and absolutely divine! This is a real treat for any chocolate lover – you could use chocolate with 70% cocoa solids or milk chocolate, depending on your preference. For an adult version add a good glug of Coole Swan Irish cream liqueur and no one will be any the wiser...

MAKES 4 MUGS

300ml (½ pint) cream

150g (5oz) plain or milk chocolate (at least 70% cocoa solids), broken into squares

350ml (12fl oz) milk

1–2 tsp caster sugar (optional)

25g (1oz) mini marshmallows

a little finely grated chocolate, to serve

1 Whisk 4 tablespoons of the cream in a bowl until softly whipped and set aside.

2 Put the chocolate in a large heavy-based pan with 4 tablespoons of water and melt on a very low heat.

3 Put the milk and the rest of the cream in a separate large pan set over a medium heat and bring almost to the boil.

4 When the chocolate has melted, pour in the milk and cream mixture and whisk continuously, until smooth and frothy. Stir in sugar to taste – this will depend on the type of chocolate you have used.

5 Pour the hot chocolate into mugs and add a spoonful of the softly whipped cream to each one. Add some marshmallows and a little grated chocolate to serve.

Festive Pomegranate Mojito

A refreshing cocktail that's sure to go down a treat. If you've got the time, freeze tiny mint sprigs and pomegranate seeds in ice cube trays topped up with water. This would also work brilliantly with cranberry juice.

SERVES 6–8

300ml (½ pint) pomegranate juice

juice of 4 limes

100g (4oz) golden caster sugar

15g (½oz) fresh mint, leaves stripped off

250ml (9fl oz) white rum

1 litre (1¾ pints) soda water

175g (6oz) ice cubes

pomegranate seeds, to decorate

lime slices, to decorate

1 Put the pomegranate juice, lime juice, sugar and most of the mint leaves in a large jug. Crush the ingredients together with the end of a rolling pin to release the flavour of the mint and dissolve the sugar.

2 Add the rum and mix well, then top up with the soda water and plenty of ice, stirring until well combined. Pour into tall cocktail glasses and decorate with the rest of the mint leaves, the pomegranate seeds, and the lime slices to serve.

Santa's Little Helper

This might be just what you need on Christmas Eve, when you've still got presents to wrap and the special china to sort out, not to mention all the other things on your to-do list. Coole Swan Irish cream liqueur is made just up the road from me by my good friend Mary Sadlier.

SERVES 2

8 tbsp cream

5 tbsp Coole Swan Irish cream liqueur

5 tbsp vodka

2 tbsp amaretto

about 50g (2oz) crushed ice

ground cinnamon, to dust

freshly grated nutmeg, to dust

Put the cream, Coole Swan, vodka and amaretto in a cocktail shaker. Add a good handful of crushed ice and shake until thoroughly combined. Strain into Martini glasses and give each one a light dusting of cinnamon and nutmeg to serve.

Index

muffins, 106

mulled wine, 220

mulled winter berry Victoria sponge, 168

mushroom and chestnut soup, 21

mushroom strudel, 155

n

non-alcoholic drinks, 7, 16, 219

nuts, 11, 34, 126, 192

o

oat and cranberry cookies, 200

olives, 11, 192

one-pot harissa turkey and butternut squash curry, 124

one-tray full Irish, 105

one-tray spinach and Gruyère brunch, 117

oriental sticky duck breasts with figs, 142

orzotto, 158

p

paella, 11, 152

pancakes, 108

parfait, chicken liver, 32

Parmesan cheese, 51, 52, 60, 144, 158, 194

Parmesan risotto, 123

parties, 11, 16

party bites

    baby gem cups with prawns and mango, 212

    blinis with smoked salmon, 215

    chorizo with celeriac remoulade, 210

    mini croque monsieurs, 208

    mini frittatas with bacon and thyme, 205

    smoked trout rolls with cream cheese and red onion, 211

    sticky cocktail sausages with sesame seeds, 216

pâté, smoked salmon, 197

pavlova with raspberries, pomegranate and lychees, 162

pear and walnut salad, 138

peas with bacon, 62

pecan and maple crumble muffins, 106

pecan tart, 165

pies

    filo-crusted fish, cheese and leek pie, 150

    MacNean frangipane mince pies, 7, 8, 86

    turkey and ham pie with puff pastry, 120

Pinot Noir, 16

plum pudding, 88

poached salmon with sourdough toasts, 134

pomegranate, 56, 91, 126, 162, 228

pomegranate mojito, 228

popcorn, 191

porchetta with sautéed potatoes, 11, 144

pork, roast, 144

porridge bread with scrambled eggs and smoked salmon, 114

port, 16, 76

port and Cashel Blue gravy, 141

potatoes

    celeriac and sweet potato boulangère, 7, 8, 59

    gratin of new potatoes with parmesan crème fraîche, 51

    jacket, 8

    mashed, 54

    roast, 8, 52

    sautéed, 11, 144

potted poached salmon with sourdough toasts, 134

prawns with chorizo and garlic, 28

preparation, food, 7–8

preserved lemons, 176

prunes and sausages wrapped in bacon, 8, 65

puff pastry tarts, 166

Puligny Montrachet, 16

punch

    Christmas cranberry and pineapple, 219

    Irish whiskey, 16, 222

puy lentils, 156

q

quesadillas, 131

NOTES

NOTES

TO-DO LIST